LETTERS FROM YOUR FUTURE

LETTERS *from your* FUTURE™

Letters From Your Future

ISBN-13:978-0615708027 (Brett\Bowden)
ISBN-10:0615708021

Manufactured in The United States of America

To Mom.
Thank you for standing by me and helping me
to try to understand what was happening
as my world was falling apart.

You had your Continuation Day as this work began.

I know you can see it completed now.

I love you.

ACKNOWLEDGMENT

First and foremost I must acknowledge my main Spirit Guide... Jaipur. It is through His presence and purpose that this book came to its fruition. I owe you debt of gratitude for your persistence in getting this book accomplished. Thank you for never giving up. It was through Jaipur's presence that He and the other Ascended Masters and were able to come through me with their wisdom and love for humanity. Without Him this book would not exist as it does today. It was through Their purpose that Humanity will be elevated to new levels of love, awareness and gratitude. I deeply thank you.

Thank you Stephanie for standing by me as this story unfolded. It was strange, weird, different and very challenging at times. You were able to keep an open mind through it all and I watched you grow as I was growing. It was just as beautiful to witness your spirit grow, as it is just to witness the beauty you embody. It is beauty from the inside out as it should be. Indeed you're my Soul Mate for all times.

Thank you Hailee and Cody. I know you didn't understand what was happening. Your world was being torn apart as mine was and I know you couldn't understand why. I hope this book will help you to understand. One day you will be able to look at what happened with a profound wisdom that all things happen for a reason and this was no different. Your Soul will gain what it intended on this journey even if it doesn't make sense right now. You are two of the best children I could have ever asked for. Never give up on your dreams and you will achieve them. Remember, Dad loves you and always will.

Thank you Kara. In this, your's was perhaps the most difficult journey. Your world was ripped apart and you struggled to find a meaning and purpose behind it all. You tried to find meaning and balance from within the middle of the storm. You played a grand part in the situation that would eventually lead to these writings. Please know that all of Humanity will be blessed by what they read here. Hopefully you can see the purpose behind what was happening as you look back. I pray that many blessings will come your way.

Thank you Joanie. You entered my life as Spirit told me there was a missing piece. You helped me to complete the puzzle and I thank you for your dedication and love for all of Humanity. You are blessed with many gifts and I know this work brings joy to your heart as it does mine to say thank you. Until we meet again dear friend.

Thank you Laura. You took my hand and helped me to understand the world of Spirit. We were brought together in a strange way and I wouldn't change a thing. It was weird and wonderful all at the same time. Your continual encouragement was vital as my journey progressed. I feel so fortunate that our Souls conspired to meet during our brief stay here. Your friendship and wisdom have been such a blessing and I look forward to what may be ahead.

TABLE OF CONTENTS

PREFACE 15

INTRODUCTION 27

THE FIRST LETTER 33

THE SECOND LETTER 41

THE THIRD LETTER 47

THE FOURTH LETTER 53

THE FIFTH LETTER 59

THE SIXTH LETTER 65

THE SEVENTH LETTER 73

THE EIGHTH LETTER 81

THE NINTH LETTER 85

THE TENTH LETTER 89

THE ELEVENTH LETTER 93

THE TWELFTH LETTER 99

THE THIRTEENTH LETTER 103

THE FOURTEENTH LETTER 107

THE FIFTEENTH LETTER 111

THE SIXTEENTH LETTER 115

THE SEVENTEENTH LETTER 125

THE EIGHTEENTH LETTER 131

THE NINETEENTH LETTER 139

THE TWENTIETH LETTER 145

THE TWENTY FIRST LETTER 151

THE TWENTY SECOND LETTER 157

THE TWENTY THIRD LETTER 163

THE TWENTY FOURTH LETTER 169

THE TWENTY FIFTH LETTER 175

THE TWENTY SIXTH LETTER 181

THE TWENTY SEVENTH LETTER 187

THE TWENTY EIGHTH LETTER 191

THE TWENTY NINTH LETTER 197

THE THIRTIETH LETTER 201

THE THIRTY FIRST LETTER 205

THE THIRTY SECOND LETTER 217

THE THIRTY THIRD LETTER 221

THE THIRTY FOURTH LETTER 227

THE THIRTY FIFTH LETTER 233

THE THIRTY SIXTH LETTER 237

THE THIRTY SEVENTH LETTER 243

THE THIRTY EIGHTH LETTER 247

THE THIRTY NINTH LETTER 253

THE FORTIETH LETTER 257

EPILOGUE 263

ABOUT THE AUTHOR 267

NOTES 268

PREFACE

I am normal.

No really, I am.

I mean really vanilla.

I'm not kidding here, I'm one of the most normal people you would ever meet. Lately though, there have been some, not so normal things happening to me, or better put ... happening through me. Let me also say very clearly that this is not my life story. That is not this book's purpose at all. This is a brief recount, of how this book came into existence. If it wouldn't have happened to me, I wouldn't have believed it, but it has happened and it is still happening and it is time for me to share it with all of you.

Let me make myself a little more clear here. Up until 2006, everything in my life plan was proceeding better than I could have expected. I was married to my best friend and high school sweetheart and very close to my extended family. I had two fantastic children who I just adored. I had a successful business. I had a house, cars, toys and everything that went along with each one of them.

However, by the beginning of 2007, I found myself going through the process of divorce, I could only visit my kids when it was my turn, I was losing my business, I was out of my house, I lost the cars, my extended family and my own family weren't acting the same toward me, my Mom's health was quickly fading away and my dog died. It was like I had been transported into the middle of a country western song and I couldn't get out. In fact, there was no way out. The problems were too big.

Through it all, I was okay. I knew, at a very deep level (one that I can't explain to you unless you have walked this walk), that everything was happening for spiritual reasons. It was something inside of me that kept me from losing my mind and assuring me that everything would eventually be okay. It was the feeling that there were reasons behind everything that happened. I knew it but I couldn't explain why. Yeah sure, I'll be very honest with you, I yelled at God, begged and pleaded and sought answers. I did all those things that desperate people do in desperate times. But somewhere, deep inside of me, I had the sense that everything that was falling apart around me had a Spiritual significance. I also later realized, as I came out of the ruins of my life, that the coming together of everything new around me also had Spiritual significance. In fact, it had more Spiritual significance than I would even understand.

In April of 2007 I filed for divorce from my wife of 20 years. I will not get into the details and reason for our divorce as I want to protect her and my children. It was soon after that time, that my business partner and I began drawing up my exit strategy, due to the divorce. Later that same year, it just so happened, that on October 31, 2007, I would find myself signing both the final divorce papers and my interest in the company over to my partner. Both on the same day.

It might not seem odd to you, but I knew that this wasn't planned this way, at least not by me. On each front, I had been going back and forth talking to lawyers, cleaning up legal language, giving concessions and preparing for unemployment. It just so happened that two of the most important things in my life, left me on that day within hours of each other with a simple signature.

Now, I realize that people go through much worse than what I have described. I don't mean to make light of situations that are far more grave than my own. But this was a big one for me and in the scope of my life it looked like my life was falling apart on every level. But really, that is where the story begins.

It was shortly after that day, that I began to wake up in the middle of the night with thoughts implanted in my mind. For the most part I never had problems sleeping, but now I found myself being woke up between 2:00 - 4:00 AM with these "thoughts" in my mind, beckoning to be written down. Thoughts like, " *Fear is the opposite of love. Fear will keep you from all that you desire to do and be while here on earth. Love however, will enable you to surpass your highest expectations.* " I didn't know how thoughts like this got there, I didn't go to bed thinking about this stuff. All I knew is that they were there and that I had to write them down. I knew they were important because of their spiritual and humanitarian theme and well, because... they weren't my thoughts, they weren't my words.

It was early in the morning on one such morning that I was told that these were called spiritual building blocks. I later discovered that these building blocks would coincide with messages that I would receive at a later time. I didn't realize it then, but as I started to put the book together years later, these "building blocks" were central themes that would be relevant to the chapter (or letter) that I would be working on. I would be in the middle of typing the pages into book form and discovered that there were coinciding "building blocks" for each of the letters that I had received years prior. These building blocks are used throughout the book and are set apart for you to meditate upon their truth and their meaning.

It was after a couple of weeks of receiving these spiritual building blocks that I started to receive other insights, other messages about the realm of Spirit and about God. These came to me as I would meditate. I had been in the practice of meditation for the purpose of clearing my mind of all the stuff that life had been throwing at me. But now, I was receiving information. Again, it wasn't me doing this. In fact, I had to get myself out of the way for the messages to come through. I had to clear my mind. I had to silence the senseless chatter of my ego that rambled on about things of little or no importance. It was almost as if I was taking dictation. As if I were receiving notes, or letters given to me in the form of thoughts that I would transcribe.

As I said, I could feel the spiritual significance about everything that was going on and the messages I would receive were something I had never encountered before with one exception. This exception took place when I was about 18 years old. I was a delivery driver and I was on my lunch break in a parking lot in Newport Beach, Ca. I had been listening to Christian radio and praying like I did most days. I had always been a seeker of God. I couldn't get enough and this followed me into my teens. This particular day, after I prayed for His guidance, I heard a voice in my head. This was the first time this ever happened. The voice said, "You will speak to my people in an another way." Whoa! What? Where did that come from I thought. I tried to ask back, "What do you mean?" The reply, "You will speak to my people in an another way." Holy !*#*! I said to myself. "Oh, sorry God" I mumbled. I'd like to say that I acquired a new level of clarity and continued the dialogue into my adult years, but I didn't. I tried, but I didn't hear anything.

I had no idea what that voice in my mind meant by what He had said. I continued on with my pursuit of God. Reading as much as I could from different perspectives. I prayed, I joined Bible studies. I took night classes at Seminary after my 12 hour days of work, just so I could get more. It wasn't until 27 years later, that I would receive a message again. And what God told me all those years ago, is making more sense to me now. What I couldn't see then, I am realizing now.

As these messages continued, I thought it was time to seek the advice of a spiritual counselor. I didn't feel this was something I could speak to a Pastor about, so I decided and felt led to consult somebody that regularly speaks to those on the other side. I had never been to a psychic or medium before, so Stephanie (the gift from heaven and the new person in my life), and I thought we would go to the bookstore and get some information about people that have the ability to speak to those in spirit. We went to the New Age section and Stephanie reached for a single book among the hundreds there. She opened the very first book she reached for and out fell a card. The card that lay on the ground was a card to a spiritual advisor. No, I'm not kidding. I thought to myself it had to be some kind of marketing gimmick. Heck, I was new to this and I thought that perhaps this is how these people operate, by placing cards inside books as though they are signs from God. I opened and shook at least fifty books that day, but no other cards were found and no new cards have been found since. Believe me, I've checked. I took it as a clear sign.

I called the name on the card, Laura Richard PhD. and made a appointment to talk to her over the phone. She acted as the medium between myself and my Spirit Guide who had been placing these thoughts within my mind. My guide told me about myself and what I had wanted to experience during this lifetime. He told me about my life plan. He told me things about myself that only I would know and things about myself that I would soon discover. He told me why things happened the way they did in my marriage and in my life. He told me that I would be writing a book or rather that he would be writing a book through me. `This is the book you now hold in your hands. My guide's name is Jaipur, he is an

Ascended Master. It is he and a collective of higher consciousness energies that are transmitting these letters during this time in our earth's history for the benefit for all of Humanity.

These messages read as letters. Indeed they were sent to me one at a time. They are brief but to the point and they address what will be happening during our earth change. They talk about how life really works and how things really are. As of now, the first book is complete and I'm writing this introduction last. It is May 19, 2008. Many of the changes that they speak of are in my future and have not taken place. So I'm taking a chance and letting them gently guide me. With all that has taken place in my life, and my full knowledge that I'm really not the one writing the messages, I do trust the information provided.

The energy that was placed within the words of this book is a loving energy. This book is meant to help those that are seeking answers to what is happening. It is meant to heal and to help those that are struggling with some of life's biggest questions. These are the reasons that you now hold this book in your hands. You see, you brought yourself here. You might not know it or understand it right now, but you were guided here, to the words on these pages and you will find the answers you seek.

These letters have been written to you, by those you can't see. They have been written out of a love that you can't comprehend right now, but it is a love that surrounds you. It is a love that has always surrounded you, even in your darkest moments. The world of Spirit is a world that is very real, a world that is full of God's love for every wonderful person including the miracle that is you. So feel the love within these words and the ideas that are expressed here. Approach this with a opened mind and see if this feels right to you. I mean really feel it and let it work through you. You already have the answers inside of you, but you need a gentle nudging, a reminder of who you are.

Put these words, these concepts to good use to make a better world for yourself, your loved ones and for all of those around you. In doing so you will create your Heaven on Earth and all will be blessed because of it.

May you create the world of your dreams.

Section 1

The Journey to Enlightenment isn't a Journey…

It's an Announcement

INTRODUCTION

Dear Ones,

We have been sending Humanity instructional letters for some time now. The Letters, collectively known as The Letters Project, started in 2007 and will continue until Humanity has reached its full potential and it is deemed that they will no longer be needed. These Letters are instructions about life and how life works from the perspective of the Spiritual Realm in which we reside.

We go by many names for there are many of us here who want to communicate these truths to you. We work through the spiritual energy named Jaipur and are collectively known to this channel as The Counsel of Divine Wisdom. We are energies that reside in the upper realms of existence. In your modern day terms you might say that we are Ascended Masters although that term you use has restrictions, but it will suffice for these purposes.

It is our intent to show you a new way, another way for Humanity to exist. Indeed, if you are pleased with what you see and feel around you, then this message will have no meaning for you. However, if you are not pleased with the present condition in which you perceive your world, then you now have a golden opportunity to change it. You can do this by changing your perception of what you see around you and in doing this you will begin to change your life, your world and yourself. This change will occur from the inside of your consciousness and manifest its way out and into your reality.

The mere perception of what you would call a fact does not make it so. It is not because you see something that it literally exist within your thought of absolute reality. A shift of thinking must occur in order for you to see your life, not through your physical eyes, but rather to view your life through your spiritual self. That is to say, to feel and experience your whole life through the myriad layers that are your consciousness. For it is you that is writhe with knowledge from the many lifetimes your Soul has encountered and the vast spectrum of experiential learnings you have walked in and through.

There is no other reason for you to have played these dramas out but for the benefit of your Soul's experience. You can choose to accept the lessons given to you or you can choose to repeat the same patterns hoping for a different outcome. By this point in your collective experience we would hope that you would make the correct decision that would move you upward in your Soul's progression and expansion and not a decision that would be restrictive with lateral progression at best.

It is here in your collective human consciousness that great truths are now being given to you. These great truths will arise from various parts of your earth, yet these great truths will be harmonious in their aperture. These truths being presented to you can be accepted by you individually or rejected collectively. Acceptance at the individual level will eventually move your collective consciousness into new realities of existence. We see this as the probable outcome at this point in your earth's timeline. However, there remains a choice for Humanity to collectively reject what is being offered for there is always a choice at hand.

By choosing in favor of acceptance, you are choosing expansion and moving into the realm of creative expression at the highest levels. To do this you must intend it. You must intend for your reality, your world to be a better place. You must intend for your world to be a world where love resonates for every human being. You must intend for this world to be safe for you and your children, for your neighbors and friends near and afar. You must intend that there is enough of what is needed on earth for every sentient being. You must intend that you live in another way that allows full expression of your individual connection with your spiritual Source. Finally, you must intend the individuation of Divinity that you are, to be expressed fully in your own life and then live in that expression.

It is in this manner of intending that shifts occur and new realities are created. It is in this manner that voids in your present lives are filled and it is in this manner that beauty is created like this planet has never known. We know the potential for human expansion is there. We can see it as you interact with each other. We can feel the thoughts and feelings you put into the atmosphere when you are in your silent times and when you gather together. We know all of it, yet the choice is not ours, it belongs to you.

We ask that you sit with these words for a while and be with them. Notice how they feel to you, for your feeling will lead you in the direction of your Soul's path. Your Soul knows which way you are to go and which way you are to grow. The world of your highest imaginings is within your reach.

It was always our intention to bring Humanity this knowledge of the creation process. We have done that successfully. What will you do now? What will you do for your your earth, for your children, for your neighbor and most importantly, for your Soul?

One such enlightened Soul wrote this and it speaks to this present moment, "*...I shall be telling this with a sigh. Somewhere ages and ages hence, two roads diverged in a wood, and I - I took the one less traveled by. And that has made all the difference*." Robert Frost

Where will your road take you? Which path will you take? Go inside yourself and seek the insights of your Soul in the silent moments. It will know the way.

THE FIRST LETTER

This is where we begin. A practical guide for understanding what is happening in the reshaping of your planet.

Things have been as they always have, until now. Now is the dawning of a new era, a era in which man will become more like he was in the beginning, when God and man breathed as one. No longer will the wall of separation divide the two. For the barriers are being broken down, even as these words are being written.

The day that is at hand is a day in which the highest imaginings of man will be realized and the hearts of all mankind will once again be reunited with the Creator. It is a day that has been foretold, it is a day that has been anticipated and feared. But there is no fear in the perfect love of God. While the scribe and the prophet both look forward to the present moment, the proud and the rebellious tremble. In reality, both are the same, a human playing the game of Humanity in a world of their own creation.

It has long since been written about a day in which a well-spring of spiritual thought would permeate the earth and that day is now upon us. This has allowed for the well to spring forth in its abundance and those that have their hearts and minds prepared will reap the benefits. Those that have their consciousness set upon the ego, will be those that are lost.

Standing upon a path of unbridled experience is where those that live in the moment of now find themselves. Eager to return to the heart of God, their experience will rush over them as a rush of cool Autumn wind. It will not be easy for those that lack in this experience to stand idly by and witness the process. In doing so, the appearance of lunacy will be misconstrued with the elation of Divine oneness. But given the opportunity to experience the Divine, it is a experience that cannot be compared to anything substantive on your planet at this time.

So it is here where we begin. It is here where this writer begins his journey to a place of unparalleled and unprecedented grander. It is a place where this writer has only imagined, but he is being taken by the hand and led to the scenic viewpoint that overlooks the panorama. Walk with us now, take this journey with us as we travel across new landscapes and view life from new vistas. It is the journey your heart aches for, it is the experience of your lifetime in a way you have always dreamt your life to be. For this is how it was meant to be, and it will be if you let it.

There is nothing you have to be but who you already are. There is no place you have to go but where you are now.

That is where the magic resides, that is where the dreams are fulfilled inside this wonderful creation that has been reunited in full measure with its Creator.

As you know, there has been a falling away, a purging if you will, of Humanity that left a negative charge upon those that sought the positive aspects of their incarnation. Do not fear for those that have departed, for they have not "died" as you have imagine death to be a permanent resolution. They have merely changed form and watch from the sidelines as you continue on your journey home, only to meet up with them again in grand reunion.

Sorrow is a natural gauge of the human condition and should be allowed its full process. In doing so, you allow healing to begin and to continue. With those departed Souls removed by their own higher choice, there remains a remnant that are contemplating the ramifications. It is not a easy process for them as they are dealing with much sorrow. Those remaining on this plane that are of a higher awareness and a high consciousness, know that the end has not come upon us, but the birth of a new beginning.

These words are being written well before the events that we speak of. It is now November 14, 2007. We note this at this time to bring validity to the message we bring forth. While we sympathize with those that have had to say goodbye to those that they loved, we rejoice with those that are left behind with the abilities afforded to them to reach their highest destinies.

The process that has occurred is a process that is very natural in the process of life itself. Life sustains itself by protecting itself from elements of danger. This can be witnessed in a wide variety of settings. The body itself, rids itself from infection through this very process. The earth, the universe and all galaxies are nothing more than a larger, albeit complex arrangement of cells, veins and arteries. They inhale and exhale with the very life force that the human body does.

So while we understand and empathize with the loss that so many have endured, we speak to you now as a method of consoling you. We again need to emphasize that your loved ones are not lost. They have been removed by their Higher Self for reasons that suited their Soul's growth. Thus, we encourage you to remain steadfast in your awareness of the occurrences that surround you and note, that in the larger scheme of things, all things are as they should be.

Those of a higher consciousness understand and are aware of this. That is why you are here. It is by the determination of your Higher Self to remain through the transition period. For your Soul will find the growth in seeks in the days, weeks and years to come. Keep yourself centered and let the God of your understanding find its place within your core. Place your trust in your Source and know from a place deep within you, that you have been brought to this place, in this time, for a reason. That reason will be different for each one of you, but the reason still remain in the light of the present occurrences.

We say that our bringing you these Letters has a place within your life right now. The words contained in these Letters offer you choices and worthwhile pieces of advice that can simply transform your present way of approaching the way you do things. We believe you are ready to take these choices and analyze them, for you are ready to consider that we have brought you something of value for you now.

In order for you to regain your way of living in a happier and more peaceful way, we suggest you bring over a loved one to your side. We suggest you make room in your schedule so that you can see and read these words very clearly. Although you might think you are seeing clearly, you may not be. We suggest you bring over a lamp or light source so you can see each word. For each word on each page brings forth tremendous power and energy for you.

You will notice that the time in which it takes to read this literature will depend on how much time you have set aside for yourself. If you wish to open yourself to this new way of looking at life, then you might consider setting aside more time for this project. If you cannot or do not wish to set aside more time, you will find that the process takes a bit longer. All in all, you will see that for those who choose to spend great time here with these words, they will benefit greatly and will grow and change at a more rapid rate.

First, we would like to thank those of you who have come together for the purpose of reading our words. We are delighted to know that you wish to know us and learn from us. We see you are enthralled by the possibility that there might be other forms of life outside your physical world. We see many who do not believe this, yet you are the few who have chosen to look outside your present state to consider other possibilities.

However you conceptualize us, we are here to guide you and show you that it is possible to love another as yourself, find love in all things, grow as a flower would blossom, and deepen your understanding of All That Is. We wish for you to know that we believe you are all students and makers of dreams. We wish for you to see that all is Divine and our presence is that of Godlike images that sit above and beyond you, as well as within and around you.

All is a tremendously powerful journey into yourself, and you will find that the path within is easy to locate and walk onto. Together, we can journey to your path and start walking on new pavement stones so you can see how a new way of life might feel for you today.

We give you these Letters for your enjoyment and for your deep concern about each other's wellbeing. If you wish to find pleasure in these words, find that they have been transmitted with loving care and good intentions. If you are reading this because of your great concern for yourself and your loved ones, please know that our hearts extend to yours and we know of your pain and your sorrow. It is with this knowledge that we can understand, that all life, both seen and unseen, is in the eternal hand of God. Your loved ones are in no danger and they know no lack and they too are in a cocoon, a protective shell of love where their Higher Self has found what it longs for.

Be at peace that our hearts are joined now as we walk you through the Letters. Our hearts beat at the same moment as we watch you pour over the material we present to you. Never forget that our hearts are joined as you partake in this journey to learn how you can find Love and Happiness and Joy again.

We wish you many blessings on this fabulous and remarkable journey you are about to embark on. The beauty of your Souls resounds through the Heavens and we feel your yearning to be seen in all your glorious beauty. Know we are with you, dear ones with loving thoughts, always. Underlying all that has happened, is the ever-present Love of God that permeates all. This understanding is at the forefront of all that has transpired and is the base understanding upon which all other understandings will be built upon. It is with this knowing that we find the strength and determination to move on and to move forward.

So take heart and use these words as a salve for your Soul, God is in full control, He loves you, He cares for you and He will not ever leave you.

Even now.

Especially now.

THE SECOND LETTER

To embrace all that has been given you, all that is required is your attention. Perhaps this is the most difficult part of all. Attention takes focus and what we are talking about here is the attention to focus. Most of your planet is inundated with noise. Noise from traffic, both in the air and the ground, children, people *en masse*, works of construction and all manner of man-made noise. Is it any wonder that so few have found the blessing that comes within the moments of silence?

Implementing the changes discussed here will perpetuate spiritual growth and foster healing on your planet.

Let's start by taking our first steps. Let's start by putting one foot in front of the other and before you know it, your journey to your center will have begun.

Find a place that feels good to you. Find a place that is relaxing. Find a place where the sounds that touch your ears are soothing. Relax in the moment, get comfortable and make yourself at home, for when you are relaxed you are at home.

Breathe deeply, exhale slowly. Let the energy that is contained within all ether cleanse you as you drink in its vibrancy. All that is needed is a few breaths to let the healing energy infuse your Spirit. This is nourishment for your Soul. This is what life is made of, literally. This is what calms you and brings you to your center and your center is where you need to be.

Focus your attention on nothing in particular. Let the dominating thoughts go. Let them gently float away and let the silence wash over you like waves gently lapping at the shore. In this silence, during the process is where you and God become one. It is not that you are never not one, but in this elevated state of focus is where the experience becomes real, where it takes its most intimate form.

It is in this space that communion at your deepest level transpires and where growth is realized. It is within this space of emptying yourself that you allow God to come in and commune. It is at this deepest level where you fuse your energies and become renewed.

Is it any wonder that Man has felt the division from the Divine presence? Is it any wonder that Man has become frustrated with his life for not working out the way he wanted it to? Is it any wonder that this frustration perpetuates itself until it develops into a deeper form of negative energy? And we look back through the eons of time and we wonder what happened.

What happened was not our longing for the Divine to interject Itself into our life. For in truth, or longing, or better put, our intention, is the only reason we have any measure of the Divine that resides with us. No, what happened is that Man has stepped away from his Creator. Man has become preoccupied in the daily occurrences in his life that he has little time for anything else. This inexhaustible conquest for more material possessions has driven Man to the brink of despair. It has culminated in a profound loss of his true identity and purpose.

Instant gratification is a poison that has injected itself upon your planet placed there by the needs of the ego to have control.
Those who are aware understand the necessity that patience is part of the Divine quality that is constantly being developed within you, bringing you closer to your Source by the very fact that patience is enacted.
What is being developed by patience is trust.
Trust that your Source will provide for you.
Trust that your Source hears your request.
Trust that the Source-Of-All-Things is present and active in your life.

It is through this refinement of trust between you and your Creator that you are being brought closer to God.

Man has taken his focus off of his relationship with his Creator and placed his focus on material goods and possessions. And again, we wonder why God seems so distant and we seek to fill the void that is missing in our life with stuff we buy to make us feel better.

Hear us now when we tell you that there is nothing, nothing that can replicate or replace the oneness, the communion that one can find with the Creator. It takes nothing to buy it. It only takes your desire for it to be so and the time given to it to let it transpire.

It is a new time. It is time to put away the childish things and time to take steps toward your spiritual maturity. This is not a call to disregard all material possessions, but this is a call to place your priorities in order. What we are encouraging you to do is to take advantage of the opportunities that have been brought forth in these days.

What we are seeking is what Humanity is seeking and we are merely pointing the way. We are telling you that from our vantage point, we can see that you have been far too busy and too reluctant to dedicate the time necessary for anything except your self-indulgent pleasures and your material possessions. Give it up and return to your Source now. Return now to your center, to your unique God-space that resides within each one of you. For in doing so, you move yourself forward in your Soul's growth and you elevate the larger part of Humanity along with you.

Developing your ability to quiet your mind is essential to the process.

This is the area you need to work on. For the most part God does not scream, but God works within the silence. All of nature continues on in silence. The planets rotate and find their alignment in the silence and miracles are performed where no words are needed. But it all starts with silence. It all starts with fine tuning the ability to hear the voice of God.

Be silent and let God present Himself to you in ways beyond your ability to foresee at this moment. Let God take you by the hand and lead you into areas that you only thought were unreachable. If you dedicate the time, if you release all thought and empty yourself, God will make His home in your heart if the space is prepared. This is what you can do. This is what you must do to continue on this journey.

Travel light because where you are going, little is needed. The heavier your load, the more you will be weighed down by it. So much so, it can prevent you from moving forward at all. Without hesitation, begin to take the first steps on your journey with us. Take your first steps moving you forward on your path.

The ideas expressed and the methods employed are not the only methods for reaching your destination or beginning your journey. Indeed, many of you have moved beyond this and into higher forms of communication, but these are the sure steps guided by the loving hand of the Creator drawing Himself nearer to you. As a child moves with anticipation and excitement into the loving arms of the parent that awaits him, so you too, run to the open arms of the Creator as She longingly awaits to embrace Her creation.

Go now, let go of all the things you have used as a crutch to support yourself and fall into the embrace of the Divine.

The Third Letter

You and all you were ever created to be was His expression of Divinity itself. You are a small individualized part of the larger whole of Divinity. As a grain of sand is of the same elements that make up the seashore, so are you of the same essence of your Divine heritage. That is why, when service to the Soul is denied, there is a void that must be filled. There is a longing to be whole again. To fill this void and to sooth this longing many things have been substituted. But none will suffice.

Home is not where your heart is -
Home, your real home, is the realm in which your Higher Self resides.

This is because nothing can take the place of the Divine, that part of you that is missing, or that part of you that has been put away. We have focused on the first steps to becoming whole again. In becoming whole, we find and release the Divinity inside of us at our core. That is your core. At your core you are Divine. That aspect of Divinity that represents itself as you seeks to experience itself as you and through you.

Does this mean that you are God? No, it does not, but it does mean that your are an individualized aspect of God realized here on earth. It does mean that you reflect God in your incarnation. That is what was meant when the Scriptures say that man was made in the image and likeness of God. It goes much deeper than previously thought and what was previously accepted. Whether you choose to accept this can make all the difference.

This is the beginning of a new version of yourself. This is a new higher version of the old Self and it is entirely of your own creation. Yes, you can take this as far as you would like and reach destinies far beyond what you thought possible. If you are willing, it will come. If you set your intention upon it, it will manifest in the physical.

What we are telling you is that in no uncertain terms, you are made in the image and likeness of God, in all that those words entail. Accept this truth as your truth. Embrace this knowingness and rejoice in the fact that this day has come upon you.

That individualized part of you that is God, that version of yourself that is your Higher Self has brought you here, to the words on this page at precisely the right moment. You were drawn here, not by chance but by Divine will, your Divine will to be and experience yourself as you know yourself to be.

Follow this urging. It is where you were meant to go. It is the direction in which you are to travel on the journey you have already embarked on. This is your map. Let your Soul guide you through this process, it knows where to go. It is your job to feel it and to respond. You are equipped to do this very thing. Your body has acute sensory receptors. They are known as your feelings. When one says he has a gut feeling about something, he is correct. These are his sensors, his feelings letting him know that he is headed in the correct direction or if he is off course. Listen to what your Soul is telling you.

Your feelings are your internal guidance system. Listen to them and they will safely guide you to your destination.

Listen carefully and trust in yourself for you are one with the Divine. If you trust in yourself, then you trust in Divinity itself. If you do not have the courage to trust in yourself, then that speaks volumes about where you see yourself and your connection to Divinity. When this takes place, you are creating a wall of separation between yourself and the Divine. You are re-creating the separation that Humanity has just walked away from. You are giving up your Divine birth-right in exchange for a man-made version. The choice is yours. The choice has always been yours and your world will always be as you create it to be.

So then, choose the path that will lead you to your highest vision of yourself. With every decision, you are creating your world as you want it to be. Until now you have been unaware of this fact. With any choice of great significance, make the choice that reflects your Higher Self and the Divinity that resides within you. Choose wisely and you will not be disappointed.

Each step taken on the path leads you in a direction. All roads lead Home, so have no fear that you can do anything that will keep you from returning to your Source. But the route that you take can and will be affected by the choices you make. This will always be your experience. Let the Divinity within you lead the way and let that Divinity within you take you on the excursion of a lifetime. In reality, that's what it is, the journey of your lifetime. Relax and go with it.

Fear is the opposite of love.
Fear will keep you from all that you desire to do and be while here on Earth. Love, however, will enable you to surpass your highest expectations.

Be well and without any fear and let your inner feelings guide you to the place you most desire to be. Follow the path that is laid before you. Listen to what your internal guidance system is telling you. Do as you wish, but always do what you wish. Your wishes will always come true given the proper energy and intention. Let this be your grand adventure. Let yourself relax into it and don't be afraid to take the hand of Divinity as you travel into unchartered and previously unknown territory.

God awaits you and will be with you and beside you every step you take.

THE FOURTH LETTER

Let us go back now and take a look at why you do what you do. Why your life is the way it is now. You have been creating your reality all along. Some of you may know this, some of you may not. Most don't realize they are doing this very thing with every thought that they send out into the universe.

Your entire cosmos is made of energy. It is all energy at different levels of vibration. Everything your eyes see is energy vibrating at different levels. When energy vibrates at very high rates of speed, the energy becomes invisible. When energy vibrates at a slower rate of speed, it becomes dense and takes on physical characteristics. Thus, everything you see on your planet is nothing more than energy vibrating at different rates of speed. These different rates of speed account for the myriad forms of matter on your planet.

Items that you thought were inanimate, like the earth you stand upon, rocks, metals and other such items are actually alive with the energy of the universe. This can be proven with the assistance of a high-powered microscope. When the aforementioned items are broken down to the microscopic level and examined, every particle under examination will be moving. They will be vibrating. There is movement in everything. There is movement in every portion of life. That is because there is nothing that is made up that is not made up with the very stuff of life - energy.

This is also true of the intangible aspects of life that your eyes cannot see. The forces upon your planets that keep them in perfect rotation and alignment, the forces that reside within your planet and the forces that effect you in everyday life all are variations in forms of energy and energy fields.

The very thought transmission that was used to communicate these words to the writer is energy. Thoughts are pure energy. This must be understood as a basic principle. It is foundational and elemental upon all aspects of your consciousness. This is how and why we say that you have been creating your life.

When you think a thought, you send out a vibratory pattern into the universe. Like throwing a pebble into a pond, the ripple effect is felt throughout the energy matrix of the universe. The energetic thought pattern combines with other thought transmissions that have the same frequency. This, as you have come to know, is the Law of Attraction. This is one of the operating Laws of the universe. Much like gravity, it is operational at every moment of your existence, whether you know about it and whether or not you agree with it. It is there and ever present in your life.

You will not understand God as He really is until you understand life as it really is. The two are one and that is one of God's greatest gifts to you.

This is how God, the Source of All Things, created it to be. It is by this method that God gives you His greatest gift - to create and experience your life in whatever manner you desire it to be. That is why it is often said that every act is an act of self creation. Every thought you send out reaches out into the universe seeking corresponding thoughts like a magnet through the Law of Attraction and drawing them back to you.

The Law of Attraction states in it's most simple form, "Like-kind attracts like-kind." For this reason, when you project a thought, a desire, an emotion, it is sent into the universe seeking like-kind transmissions of energy. The power and intensity of each broadcasted thought might be altered by the sender. This is accomplished through the power of your emotions. A thought projection infused with the power of emotion is the most powerful one can transmit.

This can be used for your benefit or to your disadvantage, for the Law of Attraction does not differentiate between good thoughts or bad thoughts. A bad thought, charged with negative energy can just as easily find like-kind thoughts in the universe and return to you and manifest in your physical reality.

In either case, you are creating your own reality with every thought. You can alter your very life experience by altering your thoughts. You can alter your life's experience by adding emotion to these thoughts. You can go even further by adding clarity to your thoughts. By being clear, by visualizing the detail you are now creating by intention. You are intending a desired result or outcome. You are no longer living your life by default. You are no longer living your life in a reactionary mode with your life being dictated by the thoughts and creations of others. You have empowered yourself. You have taken the reins of your own life and set the your course upon the destination of your own intent.

You have always had choice in the matter. God's gift was always yours. It is how He is designed to be. Even if you didn't know that this magnificent gift was embedded within you. Now you know. Now you have been taught about this portion of Divinity that resides within you. You brought yourself here for this knowing.

God desires that you experience yourself as a powerful creator, in the image and likeness of your Source. In doing so, you embrace and strengthen that aspect of Who You Are. Who You Are is the human element of

God - individualized. In this, God gets to experience Himself in you, as you and through you.

May you now clearly see that you have the power of creation hardwired within you. May you now focus on the positive aspects of life, focusing on them intentionally. Aspects of life like love, charity, compassion, hope and abundance. With focus on the positive aspects of life, with your emotion added and your consistent intention set before you, you will draw those very things to you like a magnet. You cannot help to do this, as it is an operating principle of the universe.

The difference between what you deem
success or failure
is the magnitude of your thoughts.

The level, shape or form in which the energy returns to you will be of infinite variety. This is because your energy will spring forth from you and interact with other similar energies. These other energies will have similar qualities to yours, but they will have different magnitudes imbued with their own particular emotion, power and intention sent by its senders. This happens in its most sublime forms within the energy matrix.

It returns to its sender always. It may however return to the sender in a way, shape or form that is completely unexpected or unanticipated. Rest assured, you will get what you desire. You may not get what you ask for, if the asking is not heart felt or if the asking does not resonate with the energy of emotion. But what you desire, what you focus on, what you deliberately intend on a consistent basis will be drawn to you.

Now is the time of new beginnings. Now is the time to create deliberately. Now is the time to create with intention. Now is the time to embark on your new beginning to create your life as you always desired it to be. Design your life as you desire it to be. Don't let others design it for you. Take the reins of your journey and create the grand experience that you have always desired - life as you always wanted it to be.

This is God's gift to you. Use it and experience your own creative power, the power that God gave you that is resident within you.

The Fifth Letter

When culminating your energies with preferences other than your own, extreme discretion must be observed. The forces that avail themselves to the incarnate are many. Some discarnate energies seek a vehicle in which they can make themselves known and heard. Extreme caution is urged in summoning voices or energies to help guide you on your path.

What is central to your development at this time on your planet is the understanding that you are the captain of your own ship and that you are in full control of every aspect of your journey. In these times in which you live, it is allowable to have the non-physical assist you in areas and aspects of your life. Indeed, we provide guidance and understanding to the times at hand, but what we are stressing here is the caution and use of lower energies that seek an opening, a vehicle to voice their own understanding and opinions. Understandings and opinions that are centered upon something other than your best interest. You have the power within you to solve any problem that befalls you. Deep inside you is the Source of all wisdom. Resident within you is that aspect of Divinity that is wisdom and the treasures of the universe are held within.

It is only necessary to look into yourself to find the answers. Meditate upon the areas of concern, releasing all worry and doubt and let the insight and wisdom come to you. You do not need to go anywhere. You do not need a particular person to help you with your areas of concern. You have all you need resident within you. Now we do understand that seeking outside council will make you feel better, and feeling better is a large part of the solution to any problem. What we are saying here is that the actual answers to any situation before you are held within you for your discovery despite the appearance otherwise.

When seeking to look inside yourself for the answers that lie within you, surround yourself with white light. Picture yourself surrounded by the white light of your loving Father. Summon the Angels and Guides that are for your Highest Good. In your mind or out loud, require that only those present and available to you are for your Highest Benefit.

When you hear the voice within your mind with words and concepts that are not your own, then you know you have established contact with the non-physical.

Do this often and get to know your Angelic messengers as they commune with you. Remember, you require nothing. You have all the answers you seek. However, these Guides are always available to you, whenever you wish. It is their pleasure to interact with you. That is their function, both here in your physical reality, and in the non-physical.

By calling forth these energies that are for your Highest Good, you alleviate the potential for other discarnate energies to voice their opinions led by their ego. What is available to them as a vehicle does nothing to suit your Higher Purpose. Ask them to leave, insist that they leave and they will. It matters not what their opinions or views are. What you are seeking is an abundance of wisdom that will be made known to you by those that know you best. Just as in life, you would not allow uninvited strangers into your home with access to your most guarded possessions, so also in the area of your spirit you do not allow unwelcome energies upon you to do as they wish.

The method of seeking your inner wisdom is the course and the reason you have set yourself upon the physical plane. You seek to experience and to know yourself within this realm. Divine guidance is always available to you, but exponential growth is available to those that find the treasures that reveal themselves to the heart that is open for inspection and retrospection. This is your journey, not your Guide's journey. A Guide is meant to only be that - a Guide. You are the sole energy that took form so that you might experience your Soul's growth within the physical.

Consider asking your Guides, equal to that of pulling off the road and asking for directions to get to your destination. They can tell you how to get there, but they won't and never will get in the car and drive for you. They won't and never will tell you what to do. That alone is your decision. There might be several routes to your destination, but the route that you ultimately choose, will be that of your own decision.

The most expanded and deepest growth available lies in the development of listening to your inner voice. To listen to what your Soul says. To listen to what you feel about a certain situation. This is where real growth is attained. It is not listening to a Guide and obeying. It is searching for the answers placed inside of you and following your inner truth. Is it better to pull off the road for directions every time you need to go somewhere, or is it better to become familiar with the landscape and thus plot your own course to your destination? Without question, we state the latter.

With regard to your journey, we request that it continue to be your journey. As Guide's we will always instruct you for your Highest Benefit, and we are instructing you now to find the answers you seek inside of you, not to a place that is external to you. We will be here always to guide you, but for your own Highest Highest Good. We respectfully request that you begin to look into the treasure that is waiting to be discovered inside of you.

THE SIXTH LETTER

When you were one with your Creator, you breathed as one with God. You actually lived in the knowingness that everything around you was God. You knew that there was nothing, no-thing, that was not God. It was "world idyllic" and you were in full co-creation with God, using His gifts to create a world of untold wonder. God gave you the earth to manage and maintain, and in return, the earth would provide for all of your necessities. It would ensure that all of your provisions were met.

Now, as you can see, things are far from what they were meant to be. Your separation from your Creator, and thus from your true Source, has led you down a road of poverty. Poverty of Spirit and poverty of the Source of all that you would need to ensure your survival and the survival of the delicate ecosystem. There are no rules that you have broken, for there are no rules that you must obey, but you have turned aside from what was best for you and followed your knowledge directed by your ego. You have thus encountered a disconnect with the Source of all wisdom and strength.

A course correction is needed at this point in human history and in the life span of your planet. And that is why you have chosen to incarnate at this moment in time. It is why you have brought yourself to these pages, to set the course straight and to experience the grand reunion of your body with your Higher Self. Life was never meant to be the struggle that you have created it to be and you have come to make the necessary adjustments that bring alignment to these forces.

By following the instructions given here and in the ensuing pages, you will do much to align your energies with that of a course that was designed to bring you your highest inspirations and creative abilities. By embodying the energies, you recognize yourself to be at one with all and your Creator. It is through this process of spiritual maturation that this development will occur.

Accelerated development and utilization of your spiritual gifts is commonplace and is expected in this day and age.
What is considered normal today, was once considered occult, or only for the most Holy to participate in.
They were using the same spiritual gifts, but one was revered for it and the other was put to death because of it.
It is all a matter of perspective.
Today however, Humanity has matured and moved beyond their infancy. Utilize your gifts from God and realize the Divinity placed within you and be grateful for it.

With the proper pieces in place, your civilization will once again rise to the level of spiritual attunement that it sought throughout the drought that has plagued your planet for millennia. This is not to say that there have not been avatars, icons and learned men and women sent to you at times past. Indeed, there have been, but once again the egocentric human has sought to twist, turn and control those beings. They have sought to manipulate their words, to make them a source of power for their own benefit. Now, in this new stage of development on your planet, the avatars and gifted among you are many and the teachings are vast. So fast will be the development of those that seek awareness, that the rate at which one learns will be startling.

While the tendency might be to learn from the behaviors of the past, that method will only show how you and those on your planet have arrived where they are today. A look back will be a lesson in what not to do, more than it will be a lesson on how to proceed. Yes, there are lessons to be learned from your past, but for the most part, they are not lessons that your world desires to bring into your future. You will not develop the tools you need to move forward by looking at where you have been. The past is better served as a tool of remembrance as you create your tomorrows in the Holy moment of now.

Your starting point for building your tomorrows begins in this very moment. It is in this moment of now that your power of intention, to create as you wish, resides. It is at this point that you take everything as it comes and you accept it as it is. It is the sublime that begs to be noticed here. Life is made up in the nuance of the seemingly mundane, but yet comes together as a rich woven tapestry. Your job is not to pull the threads of the tapestry to see if it will unravel. No, your job is to look into the tapestry of life and accept its perfection. Your job is to study its intricacy and to see that you fit in perfectly. You must notice that all your challenges and your perceptions of failure have their place within the rich tapestry of life. No, your job is not to resist the challenges that are brought to you, but to accept them for what they are - grand learning experiences that will move you ever deeper into your Soul's growth.

This certainly does not mean that you have to stay with the challenge that entangles you now. As we have stated before, you always have choice in the matter. But we are saying to notice the lesson in the challenge. If you desire to move away from this challenge, then make the clear intention to do so. Notice the lesson, then let it go. This is the quickest and most effective way to move through an experience that is not to your liking. Should you choose to stay and fight the challenge, you will add energy to it. In turn, it will draw more like/kind energy in the form of experiences to it, and you will find that you are unable to escape from these types of situations. This is because your resistance has magnetized the energies and they are returning to you.

An adversarial position to a problem will perpetuate the situation, by drawing negative energy to it, rather than eliminate it.

Once you learn the lesson brought to you by these experiences and you let it go and release it, you absorb the lesson and demagnetize the energy embedded within the elements that constituted the challenge.

There is a saying that is very relevant to what we are talking about: "What you resist persists, and what you look at disappears." That is, it fails to provide the power it once had over you when you added energy to it by resistance. Note that resistance is just another form of energy, and what we have told you that you must remember as a base understanding is that "everything is energy." Can you begin to see how this energetic concept is playing itself out in your everyday life? Can you now begin to see how you can eliminate some of the negative patterns that you have brought to yourself? Can you begin to see that with a simple shift in your awareness you can begin to attract more positive aspects into your life, rather than attract the elements of negative energy?

There are those who stand by and refuse to embroil themselves in a situation of a negative energy exchange.
These are the ones that have a keen sense of the universal workings of the planet and they are those that have the ability to use this gift for ultimate healing and benefit.

With this simple shift in awareness, you can not only begin to reshape your life, but you will begin the process of reshaping your planet. The very positive energy that you transmit enters into the energy grid and coalesces with other like/kind energy giving it strength to return to you. It is also received by others who have placed their positive energy into the grid. Thus, the planet as a whole benefits from your positive influence. When enough people contribute, it can effect considerable environmental change on your planet. What your histories have shown, if nothing else, is that negative energies sent out into the energy grid, have attracted like/kind energies unto themselves, thus perpetuating the very situations they endeavored to rid themselves of.

It is when the momentum shifts from the negative to the positive that you will begin to see these changes on a global scale. It is when your momentum shifts from negative and resistant thoughts about your life that will you begin to see changes within your immediate environment. The whole is greater than the sum of its parts. Every part plays a role in its contribution to the whole. This is what is meant by the term homogenic. You are all one thing. You are all "wired" the same way. There is nothing that is done by one of you that does not affect every one of you.

It is this teaching that has been argued against. It is this teaching that has long been forgotten. It is this teaching of oneness that will heal the divisions on your planet and restore man as he was originally meant to be. It is when this teaching is once again understood and embraced that unity will become normal, rather than an abstract upon the landscape.

THE SEVENTH LETTER

Being "normal" is not what you thought it was. What you thought to be "out there" is really what life is all about. Those that you describe as "out there" could be insatiably happy living a life of their own creation. Ask them and they will tell you about their energy source. They'll tell you about their eternal spirit and their oneness with all living things. And this, many of you think, is odd behavior.

Your immediate cultural setting, developed through your larger societal perspectives, would have you believe that life is supposed to be much different than what we just described above. They would rather have you believe a number of different things based upon the society in which you were raised. Most picture an angry God that is waiting to punish you if you don't do as He asks. Others will tell you that this God can only be pleased if you do these things and petition Him in the correct manner, saying the correct words. Indeed, most throughout recorded history believe that God has some sort of requirement for them to have a real and meaningful relationship with the Creator.

There will be no proof of God that will be valid enough for the skeptic that chooses to disregard the evidences provided to him.

What has been created is a God with needs. It is a God created in the image and likeness of man, wrought with human characteristics. What we are here to tell you is that this God you have known, through your societal perspectives, is a myth. God, The Source of All Things, is indeed real, but the way in which you describe Him is inaccurate at best.

You must know that change is now upon you. Ushering in a new day in human development is the Spiritual Age of Enlightenment as it will come to be known by all. Gone are the days of hopelessness and despair. Gone are the days of selfishness, ignoring the needs of the body as a whole. Gone are the days of separation between God and Man. The Age of Man is now coming to a close.

There will be challenges ahead, but those challenges will be self-imposed. They will be brought upon the person or group transmitting the energy for the purpose of learning or experiencing a particular aspect of themselves. The difference between what has transpired in the past and this new action is that those doing the transmitting know that they are doing this. Those in the past thought that they were victims of the effects of life, not knowing that they were at cause in the matter. Those enlightened Souls, now living know they cause all they wish to experience. They also wish to experience the results of their endeavors through much trial and effort. We see the hard working Souls as learning much through this process of causing and affecting their realities. Thus, they are at full creation of the lives, as are all the rest of you. The sooner you come to know and understand this, the sooner you can begin to create a life you only dreamed was possible.

This life of dreams is not for a select few. It is for everyone. This is the exact reason you brought yourself here on this planet during the Spiritual Age of Enlightenment. That is why this is being repeated here. Because you brought yourself here to this book, to this exact page so that you can re-discover what your Higher Self already knows. Don't shrug this off. This does not happen by chance. There are no coincidences. There are reasons for everything that happens and the very reason that you are here, reading these words is because this is something that you need to know and understand. At the Soul level, you have brought yourself here to gain this understanding.

Everything happens at its prescribed place and time, but the personality can always exercise its free will option.
Going through the encounter will always produce growth, but there is always a choice.

If you are unable to continue in this process, then you must know the vibrational rate of your entire planet is rapidly increasing This is by design. This is by choice, so that Humanity can experience these higher aspects of itself. Without the acceleration of vibration, you would continue to experience life as you always have, with only a select few enjoying the benefits that heightened awareness brings. As it is now on your planet, more and more are finding the sheer exhilaration of co-creation and are in the process of designing their lives through their thoughts as they only could have imagined them to be.

Accelerated avenues of learning are available to you by your intention that it be so.

It is imperative, not only to your health and vibrancy, but to the same health and vibrancy of your planet. Those that find themselves unable to sustain the higher vibrational frequencies will find themselves with side effects of such a difference of vibrational rates. Those that are unable to sustain such rates will find themselves becoming ill and/or will succumb to the events of life. Living with the vibrational shift that has occurred and will continue to occur is necessary for the survival of your species and the survival of the planet.

Those unable to make the transition have done so at the Soul level for reasons known only to that individual Soul, but certainly it is for the benefit of the Soul's growth. Many of those Souls that have fallen away during the transition have done so to gain insight that could only be brought through the experience of a shorter incarnation during this time in human history. There are no wasted moments. Every moment is a moment of growth. Every moment spent here by those now departed was a moment of development in some form or another. While you might observe a person as wasting time, in essence there is no such thing. There is only the golden moment of now and none of those golden moments go to waste. No Soul will fail to reach the desired experience it seeks.

The Soul will not fail to experience growth during its physical incarnation.

What might appear to you as a life wasted, devoid of any enriching experiences, is actually a life granted profound spiritual insight. These insights might not be recognized as such by the personality, but all the experiences culminate in the Soul's development and growth. The personality, upon departure, will reunite with those in the non-physical and the higher aspects of itself. A life review will be engaged and the Soul will once again encounter every moment, from not only the Soul's perspective, but from the perspective of those in which the Soul participated. All of this transpires in what, in your time, would be considered a millisecond. There is no remorse offered for the things not said or done. There is no elation for the task performed well, but all information, through the sense of feeling, is assimilated and absorbed by the Soul for the purpose of growth. The Soul next decides how it would next like to approach its next adventure.

Many Souls desire to stay and teach others what they have learned. Many Souls plan new incarnations by in which they can develop higher aspects of themselves.

The Soul will never stop learning. There is always something new to experience. The Souls that develop quickly will move into deeper experiences. Most of those Souls have remained as guides to help others through their various incarnations. These guides are available to all and will incarnate themselves on occasion to interject gained wisdom for the elevation of Humanity as a whole.

When you have gained the wisdom brought to you through the lessons and experiences you planned for yourself, those lessons will leave you and new lessons will present themselves.

A spiritual master might not appear as you believe he or she would. A master is not always the one who delivers the greatest truth, although that does happen quite often. The purpose of a spiritual master is the drawing out of your own truth. A master might present himself as one who teaches absurdities. Upon contemplation of these absurdities, you come to the realization that these teachings do not resonate with you, that your feelings about these teaching don't sit well with you. You might conclude that these teachings are not in alignment with your highest good and you choose to ignore them. Through this method the master, although teaching absurdities, has helped you to draw out your most inner truth.

A spiritual master might deliver truth to you that resonates well with you. His teaching might go against what you thought you knew about life and its function and purpose. You don't know why, but at your core this feels right to you and so you embrace his teaching into your learnings. This spiritual master has also drawn out, in you, your most inner truths. Either way, you are always led back to your most inner truths and that is where the treasure is - within you.

In the end, it's not ultimately important that you follow one teacher over another. The greater lesson here is that you follow YOUR inner truth. Your inner truth will always lead you where you need to go. It will always lead you to a place of learning and developing. It cannot fail to do that.

THE EIGHTH LETTER

Attunement is the ongoing process of tuning in your vibrational frequency to that of your Higher Self, your Higher Self that resides in the non-physical. For most, it is a process that never ends. It is a journey of discovery. Indeed, it is one of life's discoveries. It is a process honed by you and no one else, for this is your journey, and yours alone.

Once this aspect of attunement can be reached, the relationship between the Higher Self and the personality will grow because clarity will be gained. With clarity, comes wisdom and insight. It is through this means that you will be able to understand the larger picture of life and your role in it. It is through attunement that you will be able to convey the thoughts from the Higher Self to the personality, thus empowering the exploration into an even deeper form of communication.

Like all other things in life, the level of attunement is only limited by your imagination. Your intention is always the key here. Your persistent and emotive thoughts about tuning into the frequency of your Higher Self, or any other energy, is your only limitation. All limitations you have are self-imposed limitations.

For some, the process might be instantaneous, but for most it will be a life-long process of the most joyous kind. Realize what you are doing here - you are tapping into your Higher Self - your source of wisdom and inner guidance. You are, over time, building a relationship with the deepest aspects of yourself and, like any other earthly relationships, it is one in which great care is needed. Like other earthly relationships, ample time is required for the development of the relationship.

On many occasions, within the framework of earthly relationships, you might get into a discussion in which you cannot understand the other's point of view. No matter what he or she says, you just can't see their point. It is at this juncture that you are talking past each other. It is at this point that it is often said that you are on a different wavelength. This is indeed true. The two of you are talking, but the receptivity to the words (which are a form of energy) are not there. You are not talking in a way that is clear to the other person.

There is no difference here. This is what we are talking about. Like all earthly relationships, communication is the key. If you don't have good communication within your relationships, at some level, the relationship will suffer. There are those who have been together for many years in which very few words are necessary, but the thoughts and emotions within the relationship are still conveyed. This is because they are communicating at a deeper level. This didn't happen overnight. It was developed over a period of time. The relationship and the communication with your Higher Self will most likely take the same turn and it will take time to develop.

The relationship you develop with your Higher Self will only be as good as the time and effort you put forth in developing that relationship. However, the insight and wisdom that you will garner from the relationship and your communication with your Higher Self is well worth any time and effort you had to put into it. Initiate the conversation and the relationship will begin. Be attentive and have the patience to listen.

The true spiritual path was the road less traveled. It is a road devoid of the ego and a road of unlimited possibilities - and that can and will make all the difference.

From the beginning, you will develop new insights about your Soul's purpose and journey and yet, this is just the beginning. You will go on to discover more about who you are at every level of your being. This is what the experience is all about at the micro and the macro level. It is about discovery. Once you discover the higher aspects of yourself, it becomes about creation. This is where the rubber meets the road. This is where you actually put your new discoveries into action and watch them manifest.

What you have chosen is no small feat, but you can do it. You are a most spectacular child of God. This is your journey.

May it be well with you.

THE NINTH LETTER

Purification was an integral part of religious celebrations and practice since man became invested in religious pursuits. It was often thought that only the most Holy of people could approach God. It was thought that these people must live lives of restraint. It was thought that these people must live lives of continuous devotion and reverence to the deities they worshipped. The slightest character flaw by an individual was thought to bring wrath upon that person. This would take the form of disease, of blindness and even death. Many times God's wrath would be visited upon the people and God was said to annihilate whole civilizations because of His anger at not following His rules and disobeying His laws.

Your pursuit of righteousness was not, and never will be, a necessary requirement for God to draw close to you.
God is always nearer to you than you can possibly imagine.

We are here now to tell you that this is not true. These are myths developed by your societal perspectives to support and give credence to whatever particular brand of religion that is being purported. You all have your perspectives within your societies. Each may have its own variance and nuance, but you do all have them. Most revolve around this idea that God is angry and that man is separate from God. That man is born sinful and unable to approach God unless a particular thing is done. Your variances are in the "thing" that must be done to please this angry God.

We will not get into naming the differences here. That has been done *ad nauseum*. We will not add to the negative energy that pits one religion over and against another. We will, however, tell you that this thinking about an angry, vengeful God is wholly and holy incorrect. God does not commune with the righteous only. God does not include one group or race and not another. This is not how God works because this is not the basis of Love. Prejudice is not an action that Love would condone. Therefore, prejudice is not an action that God would condone. This is because God is Love. These words are synonymous.

As God does not seek to keep any away from Him, He allows all to reside in His presence. There is nothing, no-thing you have to do to earn your way there. This is the glory of God that makes Himself available to all. This is because you are a part of Him. How could He then deny a part of Himself to Himself? This is illogical. This is why separation from God is a fallacy.

God loves you. You are perfect in His eyes. He sees beyond the imperfection that you and others around you see. God sees your full potential and He knows that every moment you are bringing yourself closer to that perfection. He is experiencing this journey through you. He is experiencing His creative power in, as and through you. This is how God experiences Himself. You are how God expresses Himself.

Where God resides, in the realm of the absolute, there is nothing but perfection. Therefore, God must have a way to experience Himself as something other than the perfection that He already is. You cannot experience yourself as something you already are if there is nothing else. When there is nothing else but what already is, something other than what already is, must be, in order to see what it is you are. So, God could not know Himself in the space of nothing but His pure perfection.

And so it is, in the space of what we will call absolute perfection, that the energy that humans call God, resides. For He is that perfection of incalculable grandeur, far beyond what your theologians have speculated. And it is within this Divine plan of knowing Himself experientially, that you have been brought forth. That is who you are, a Divine aspect of God. An individual aspect of God created so that God could experience and express Himself. Think carefully upon this and you will begin to understand all that you are and all that you were created to be. You are marvelous, indeed, and the grand creation of the Creator.

By being yourself in full harmony with who you were meant to be,
you display to the universe all that God is, in His experience at the human level.

It is within this interaction of God and Humanity that you have chosen to partake. It is at this junction that you are co-creating your tomorrows with God. These are the tomorrows of your highest imaginings and they will surpass your highest expectations if you choose.

All that is required is your attention to your intention.

That is the key that unlocks the door to your imaginative future... your attention to intention.

THE TENTH LETTER

While walking along your path of your own creation, be careful to note the sights to behold along the way. There are lessons for the careful observer. Every person, every relationship has been brought to you, by you. You have designed it this way so that you can learn and grow from each relationship. Each relationship holds a nugget of wisdom to be unearthed. The cumulative assimilation of the nuggets you have collected are thereby a treasure you have buried long ago, waiting until this moment in what you call time, to be rediscovered. Looking at the map of your life, plotting your course, the setbacks, the thrill of climbing to the mountaintop and eventually looking back over your journey is where you unearth your treasure.

It might or might not contain the riches of your present physical reality, but you will be much richer for it nonetheless. Although you might not have had joy and bliss in every step of the journey, you will be able to look over the terrain of your life that you have traversed with inexplicable wonderment of your achievement. An achievement not measured by human calculations, but achievement borne from the perspective of your Soul, the only perspective that matters.

All great truths present themselves within your core and work their way out into your physical reality and your realization.

With this newfound perspective, you will go on to plan other journeys, perhaps now in your physical state or upon your return. And most of you will desire to return. How can it not be? You desire to take your new learnings and expand them to even further depths and, for some, into other dimensions.

The wheel of life never stops turning. It spins endlessly, and with every rotation, every cycle it moves you closer in your ascension to the perfection and total unification with All-That-Is. THAT is where you are headed. THAT is the magnetic North that your internal compass points to. THAT will be your final destination at a point in time that is undisclosed and further away in your description of time than is calculable. But you will get there nonetheless. You will be unified with all the learnings, all of the teachings that each incarnation has given to you and each perspective that you have discovered along the journey.

You cannot fail. It is simply not possible. And as often as some of you feel like failures, if you only knew the truth of ultimate reality as we are explaining it to you here, you would realize that even your perception of failure is yet another learning, another opportunity for growth that leads you further upon your journey and ultimately, to what you would consider victory.

So, set aside all notions of failure. There is no such thing. You have nothing but success in every moment you have participated. All that is needed to see this is a new vantage point, a higher vantage point. If you could stop reading for just a moment to relax your mind and step above your problems of yesterday, today and tomorrow. Transcend them. Rise above them to a higher perspective. At an increased vantage point, you will see that, as you look back at where you have been and you look forward to where you are going, all has been necessary for the growth and development of that unique aspect of Divinity known as you. You must know that no one else can add the experience to the whole that your are uniquely situated to offer. Do you realize how incomplete the whole would be without your contribution to it? Can you begin to see now how your growth can contribute to the growth of the whole?

Humanity is all one thing divided into billions of parts, but it is one thing regardless. And what we are telling you now is that you, each of you, play a vital part in the forward progress of the one thing. So never see yourself as a failure or conclude that your life does not matter. It matters more than you can possibly know.

Take our words from our vantage point. If you were able to see the terrain that lies ahead of you and place your trust in these words- Your life and every part of it matters deeply to God. Make the best of this knowledge. Use the tools He has given to you to create the life of your highest dreams, and give thanks. You have much to be thankful for.

THE ELEVENTH LETTER

Immersion as it relates to the spiritual process is the living a life that is directed by the Spirit. It is the listening to the still small voice that guides you. It is the process of becoming acclimated to a life no longer driven by the ego, but one that is given over to Spirit - your Spirit.

You will never finish. You will never get to be completed. This is because there is always more to learn. The depths of the spiritual path are limitless. Just when you think you have reached a plateau, you will see that there are new areas of discovery. Just when you think that you have solved a piece of the puzzle, new pieces emerge that lead you further and further on your journey of discovery. This is how it should be. For you are learning about the inner workings of God. You are learning through your experiences. You are not only grasping this intellectually, but you are actually contributing to a living classroom of experience. This particular type of educational tool is one that is designed to bring you the deepest and most profound lessons. Your Soul, your Higher Self, benefits from all of these experiences of the personality.

This process of assimilation might very well move past the perception of the personality and one might wonder how anybody could ever benefit from such an experience. Rest assured, at the Soul level, all experiences bring valuable insight and learning. This is the way God, The Source of All Things, designed it to be. This is the grand design by which God, in you, gets to experience life (which is just another expression of God) in, as and through you.

When you don't live your life by false motives and relinquish the ego, you give yourself over to your Higher-Self, the true essence of who you are.

When you get to the point in which you begin to trust the God within you a little more, and you are able to relinquish the ego a bit, the process of immersion will have begun. From there, it is but a short step until one is fully immersed in the process of a life that is Spirit-filled.

The outside world would never know by casual observation, of the immeasurable changes taking place within you. As well it should be, for it is your journey and yours alone. But you will see the changes. You will notice the differences. Some of the things that were important to you will no longer hold the same importance. Some of the things that you held so close to you, that gave definition to your being, will be easily let go and replaced with things or elements that are higher in nature.

This is because the process of immersion has taken place. You are seeing life, and all it contains, from a higher perspective and a new vantage point. It is almost as if you have climbed the steep hill overlooking the dark valley, and from this new vantage point you can clearly see the road out. From this new perspective, you can see the road that you have been traveling for so long now and you can see where it intersects other major roads.

You can see, perhaps for the first time, that you have been going around in circles, traveling much, but moving very little. You can now see why you were there and what its purpose was, and you look back with fond memories and you are grateful for these experiences. You also know however, that it is time to move out of that valley of experience and into another. Another valley of a higher elevation and a higher vibrational frequency.

And so you begin to trust. You begin to trust your internal navigational system placed inside of you that will lead you through the experiences that you have chosen for yourself. And you will do this even when all outside appearances seem to the contrary. You will feel a compulsion and a leading that will defy explanation, but you will be unable to deny the very feeling that is inside of you. This is your Higher Self moving you. This is who you are and this is why you are here. Trust this feeling.

The individual that lives for the expectations of others, is the individual that has taken a longer path for the development of the Soul's growth.

This higher approach might be controversial, but it is always true for you. Your movement does not and will not make sense to others, and in the midst of it, you might find great confusion in your mind, but this is exactly why this feeling has been placed inside of you. The battles that rage within you, the battles of logic, the battles of defeat and so on, are all battles of the ego trying to control its domain.

These benefit you while living on your planet, in certain areas of your life and they are necessary. They, however, are not necessary when we discuss matters of the Spirit. You will always have free will to make decisions, and your decisions will either be made in the mind with the assistance of the ego, or they will be made in the heart with the assistance of the Spirit. The latter is the higher path that reflects your higher purpose. The former is a reflection of your life as it was, until now. The two are drastically different. A choice made in favor of your eternal purpose will move you further on your journey of spiritual development than from a decision made by pride of the ego out of its need to protect itself.

The spirit will not use force.
The free will choice of the individual is a integral part of the growth process and of the life plan itself.

In any instance in which you find yourselves at a crossroads and you can't see a clear way out, climb to that higher place where you can gain sight of the road again. Indeed, you might feel as if you are lost and there's no way out, but that is not true. You merely need to get to a place where the road is visible again. That higher place is within the realm of Spirit and is always accessible. Call upon it, feel its presence within you. It will answer you. It must, because it is you.

The process in which one becomes attuned to the guidance and instruction of the Soul and of Spirit is that of opening up. It is a giving of yourself. It is not something you do physically per se, but a inward state of being and a state of acceptance.

In this present day and age, you have these tools accessible to you more than any other time in human history. The more that humans develop and utilize the gifts placed inside of them, the higher vibration is added to the planet overall. By this positive movement of energy, your energy, you are helping to add to the overall positive energy of the planet, thus lifting up your fellow man and life in general.

We are here to tell you that you have all that you need inside of you. You have the tools in which you can make your life and life on your planet infinitely better. You will not find this by listening to your ego. You will only find this when you release your need to have things your way for your immediate benefit. You will only find this by letting go and letting you guide yourself, by letting God guide you and by trusting the world of Spirit from which you originated.

THE TWELFTH LETTER

This is the end of this leg of your journey. Like all seasoned travelers, your love for traveling, for experiencing new places, new cultures and new people will fuel your desire to have more of the same. And so it will be for you. Your desire for it to be so will make it real for you. By now, you should be able to realize this.

Your journey is not over by any measure, though. You will only rest here with your new discoveries of creation and put them to work for you. This is a time to gather your strength and to work with and within these newfound spiritual gifts. After a time, you will hunger for more, and more will be provided to you. You might even be at that point now with a keen desire to move deeper. And that is good, but recognize the opportunity that you have to put these gifts to work for you in this present moment. Don't pass up the treasure that is already yours for the hope of greater gifts. Enjoy what you have discovered. The enjoyment of this aspect of life is a tool just as everything else. The process of enjoyment itself will move you forward and deeper into the aspects of life already explained here.

We are thrilled that this communication has been established and we very much look forward to carrying on our teachings in future communications. Take a breath and look back upon the pages that have been delivered to you. You will find new truths and new perspectives built upon those truths every time you read through this material. This is our gift to you. These are timeless truths, but are only being recognized as such in this present day and age. Take these truths and make them your own. Create the life of your highest imaginings and help one another in the process. Be that very change that you desire to see in the world around you. Never forget that you are one with your Creator and that you are one with each other. Respect your differences, for there is much to learn from one another. Lastly, thank the God of your understanding for all that you have been fortunate enough to encounter.

The discoveries and teachings here will serve you and Humanity well, and that is our intention.

This is so.

Section 2

There are layers in your understanding of reality and that is what will be under examination next.

This will give you a better understanding of how life works on your planet.

THE THIRTEENTH LETTER

From the beginning of all time, life has flowed with a limited current of energy. It has been a consistent current of vibrational energy that has allowed mankind to progress in his awareness. Some have elevated themselves and have been able to ride the current into its full potential. Sadly, most go unaware of the inner workings of life and thus, live lives of quiet desperation as they wonder if this is all there is.

Now a new wave of energy is washing over your planet. It is a wave that is of a higher density - a higher and larger bandwidth if you will. Those on your planet need only to be instructed on how to use this denser energy available to them. We will note the date of 2/16/08 here. Again as a reminder that we are sending this message in advance before these changes take place.

As it is now, those of you that are more sensitive to shift in energies can already see the changes taking place, both within you and within your world. Some are for the better and some are for the worse. The better because you have found new talents and new discoveries about life. For the worse because those that are not able to make the transition are becoming more agitated and aggressive in their behavior. Both of these patterns will continue until the wave of energy fully permeates your planet. There will be dramatic changes as the higher, smoother frequency takes over the lower, uneven frequencies.

We have already noted the outcome in our first correspondence to you, so we will not cover the same material again. By now you are able to recognize that dramatic changes have occurred and are taking place. The changes are in place to bring about a certain effect. The effect will be noticed and implemented by those whose awareness is being brought forth. In our prior transmissions we have discussed many of the changes that will occur. We have instructed you on many of the basics that Humanity can and will embrace.

Your whole life reflects your spirituality, from where you shop to who you vote for. Everything works its way out from the inside and is reflected by your external actions. This will not change in this New Age of Enlightenment, but it will be brought to the forefront and the choices that Humanity will make, will be determined by their new source of spirituality as they realize the role they are here to play.

Everything in your physical existence has its starting point in your mind.

Nothing exists without it first being a thought.

Your delicate ecosystems will once again regain their former glory in a two-fold process of revitalization. Humanity will reflect its Higher Self and thus make higher choices in favor of preservation and conservation. They will make laws of protection that will cease the destruction of many of your planets ecosystems that were designed to sustain you. You will again act as caretaker of that which is meant for your sustenance, instead of acting as a destroyer as if the supply was limitless.

Your ecosystems and all living things will also benefit from the wave of energy that has swept over you. Your plants will thrive with this new energy. They will grow more resistant to disease. They will produce more of their own kind. Their produce will be healthier as the environment in which they grow will be protected. Humanity will garnish the favor of this new relationship with nature and one will benefit from the other.

Your harvests will be bountiful and that bounty will be the mechanism that allows you to feed your poor and impoverished. Lands that were once barren can and will have the ability to provide food for its inhabitants once again. This will be made possible by the heightened awareness of Humanity and the knowledge that all things are now possible when Humanity can focus its intention upon anything. You have the ability to change weather patterns and this you will do - and all of you will benefit.

"By the way you think and by the way you intend life to be... will it be." If you could have just one basic instruction for all of life on your planet, this would be it.

This transformation will not come overnight, but in relative terms, it will come quickly. In fact, the more focused energy that is provided towards a certain thing, the quicker the change. It is indeed a grand time to be alive. You are not only living, but you are discovering your tools that enable you to thrive. This is what you desired for yourself. This is Who You Are. You are now in the mode of co-creation with the Source of all living things... and it feels wonderful.

THE FOURTEENTH LETTER

We know that all of this is very new to you. We know that it sounds odd to you to hear us say that this is the experience you desired before you came to your planet. We also know that this type of thinking, for the most part, has been considered New Age and reserved for those considered on the fringe by mainline religions. The truth of the matter is that it had to happen this way. This is the only way it could have occurred. A message like this could not have come through your mainline churches or synagogues , for it wouldn't have fitted into their predetermined criteria. The message, in essence would have fallen upon deaf ears and eyes that weren't prepared to see what they didn't expect to see.

Therefore, it was necessary that the recent occurrences must take place, yes even the dramatic occurrences. It was necessary so that the message that is being brought to you will touch those that are searching for answers about life and the situation in which they find themselves in.

It often takes times of great tribulation that become the catalyst for dramatic growth and change. It often takes times of great trivial to give you the opportunity to discover what you know yourself to be. These events are such a catalyst and they will serve their intended purpose.

You might still find this difficult to believe, because at your present level of consciousness, you are unaware of the predetermined plans of your Soul. That is why we stressed in our prior communication with you, the importance of going inside of yourself and seeking that oneness with yourself. This oneness will make you whole and give you insight and clarity.

Your life will follow a prescribed course. This is of your own choosing. It was designed this way so that you can have the experience of your desire.

If you have not taken the time to do this, we ask you to put this book down, find a quiet, safe and peaceful place, take some deep cleansing breaths and let your worries subside. Let your thoughts go and connect again with your Higher Self. We know you look to these books for answers, but what we are telling you is that your answers lie within you. Therefore, it is necessary that this Soul exercise become as normal as physical exercise. What your body needs to develop and sustain itself in meaningful ways, your Soul needs the same.

Why do you seek assistance from others for your "problems?"
You are all you need. You can take care of any issue that comes your way.
You simply need to move in that direction and experience the completeness that is you.

In truth, your Soul needs nothing. It's the incarnation, the personality, that needs this particular exercise to complete itself. In many cases, this is what is meant when one says that he must "find himself." That is precisely what he is doing. He is attempting to find that "thing" that he knows that resides within him. He is seeking to make himself complete. While this is taking place individually, the collective consciousness of Humanity and its awareness of itself has been vibrationally raised and its boundaries extended further than it knew possible.

This would not be possible however, if the dramatic changes that have effected your planet would have not occurred. In essence, what we are telling you again is that, although things are not as they have always been things are as they are supposed to be. It is by design. Your design. You are the architect and the archetype of who you designed yourself to be. So live within this relational space that you have created for yourself. A space in which there are great contrasts that stand in relation to one another, but a space in which you are the bridge that joins, that heals and a bridge that brings unity to your planet.

THE FIFTEENTH LETTER

These are the times in which unity will find its place on your planet. It is the disunity of Humanity with itself and its Creator that has created the disfunction and the ensuing calamity that followed. At your essence, you are all one. You are of one mind even though you are individual Souls. Your actions and intentions at the non physical level are directed out of and through love. Love is an energy all its own.

Universal oneness is a reality that cannot be denied.
The rejection of a truth does not make it so.

With the light, smooth current of energy that has washed over your planet, your thoughts and intentions will rise and will be elevated to those of a higher nature. You will begin to see life as it was really meant to be. Your actions will be prefaced with thoughts such as: How does my action effect others? What will I learn by doing this? Will this provide positive or negative energy to the planet? You will begin to see things, situations and people from a higher perspective. From this elevated perspective you can see many things that you couldn't have before. You will be taken from the mindset of the limited to the grandeur of the limitless and you will know at a very deep level that there is nothing that you cannot accomplish given the proper focus and intention.

The power that you will derive by a unified approach will be unparalleled in your human history. A picture had been given to you already of what can happen when Humanity is not unified. Atrocities (unparalleled) had been occurring all because of this disunity. Just the opposite is about to occur and is occurring in small numbers on your planet.

This unity and infusion of positive energy will literally heal your planet. The very ground you walk on will benefit from this momentous shift in awareness. This is something that the majority of Humanity could not have known before. There had to be a planetary shift in awareness for changes of this magnitude, to even be considered, not to mention attempted. Now the time is ripe and the harvest is ready and the earth will spill forth her goodness for you; for you are once again whole.

Everything in life works its way from the inside out into your reality. This wholeness is nothing new to your Higher Self. This is just a external sign of what you already are, of what you have always been and what you took form to be. Search yourself in the silence and you will know this to be true. While it is true that you live in a universe that has infinite variety, it is also true that everything in this universe is unified. All things share their Source and there is no-thing , nothing that is not of this Source. We are merely individual aspects of the same Source. Search yourself in the silence and know that this is true. Within this truth lies great power. A power for the good of all Humanity. You need only to realize this and move towards enacting it.

You and your neighbors are one.
You are a individual aspect of God, wrapped up in different packaging.
Love and care for each other as you love and care for yourself.
In doing so you raise your vibration and the vibration of the person cared for.

We cannot emphasize enough about the strength you possess when you unify your thoughts, your intentions and your energies. This truth is the Master Key that will unlock healing at the planetary level. There can be no greater discovery than this, in which all Humanity can find and know peace. When you understand and you know, and you know that you know that all things are one thing, and that every other thing is part of that one thing, will you move towards patience and peace, and the destructive practices of the past will stop and a healing growth will begin.

What a glorious time to be alive. What great power and responsibility you have given to yourself. To know that you, where ever you might be reading these Letters, have brought yourself here, in order that you might remember who you are at your essence and that with this remembering you give yourself great power. The power to heal your planet in unity with every other person who has remembered who they are, is a plan that could only have come from the Most High - the Source of All Things and the Golden Thread that unifies All Things.

May you never look upon another with hatred, but only in love, for love is what you are and it is at this point that you come to realize that there is no "they", that there is only "us."

Search in the silence and know this is so.

THE SIXTEENTH LETTER

There are, as there has always been, those that sit on the sidelines and scoff. Those that seek an opening to ridicule to bring you down, even during the transition period in which we are now in. It is important to remember that they themselves are on their own journey. Don't pass judgment on them and condemn them for not following their higher path. Simply let them find their own way. There is no need to engage in an extended dialogue with them about the ultimate truths of life. This will only drain your energies.

All things are new again, the old has washed away.
Pay attention to your desires and your greatest dreams
will become your reality.

Your energies that can be used for other things that are more beneficial to you and to your planet. We are not suggesting that your forsake them altogether, but that you need not seek to convert them to your way. Their way will eventually be made known to them.

Your spiritual development will continue to develop at whatever pace you wish.
You have been developing for one reason and one reason only -
that at some level, you intended it to be so.
Your intention is your primary tool of development.

This time is for you. This time is for your development and for the free and unlimited exercise of your spirit. Let your past go and let go of guilt. You may use them as remembrances and stepping stones that will move you into your tomorrows. Your memories and the lessons you have learned are but a bridge that will bring you into the higher truths. Learn this about yourself and you will have learned a great truth. Teach this and you teach the great truth of eternity. For that is where you are, in the midst of what you would call eternity with its infinite lifetimes behind you in which to learn and infinite lifetimes ahead of you in which to experience.

This is the wheel of life revealing itself to you. You can enter the wheel of life anytime you desire to gain the experience you desire. You can also exit the wheel when the Soul has experienced what is desired. That is the magic of life and what a magical show it is.

It is difficult to see these truths from where you stand. A higher perspective is indeed required and that is what we are sharing with you now. The wheel of life is that in which you choose the time and space in which you would find your best choice for gaining experience would be accomplished. For some, this might be a date in the "future", even beyond the date in which you are reading this. For others this might entail venturing back into what you call "time" to grasp the learnings that only that time, location and circumstance can bring you. Your Soul, together with its Guides, make careful detail in the planning of this, so as to give to you, your highest experience. That does not always mean what you would consider a fun filled, easy or wealthy incarnation, in human terms, but it is always of the highest benefit at the Soul level.

All things culminate with your moving into the higher realms.

Your Soul uses the body as a tool in which to gain from the earthbound experience, for the Soul is pure Spirit and is formless. The Soul extracts the lessons from the physical incarnation of the body and adds them to the totality of all the physical incarnations it has accumulated. In doing this the Soul is provided with experiences from every vantage point; the rich and the poor, the male and the female, the sighted and the blind, the favored and the shamed, the guilty and the innocent. It is all included in the totality of learnings at the Soul level.

Translated into your current incarnation, this means that your life is following its prescribed course. It means that all things you thought were mistakes, were not mistakes at all, but a tool in which to learn from at the Soul level. Your economic, emotional and physical struggles were not things that happened to you, they were experiences planned by you and your Guides because, at the Soul level, you sought the experience that only these conditions might bring to you.

Your life will follow a prescribed course. This is of your own choosing. It was designed this way so that you can have the experience of your desire.

While we empathize with those that find themselves in circumstances which are very real and very difficult, we also must emphasize that these conditions were chosen by you, so that you would derive the most profound learnings from your physical incarnation. It is our intent that this revelation might not only be educational to you, but that it provides a great sense of comfort to you. We ask that you look deeply inside of yourself for revelation and for validation of this aspect of yourself. Your Soul will make it known to you. It will not only show you this, it will not only give you validations, but insights specific to your journey.

It is with this that we encourage you to look into the silence of your being to gain wisdom that you already possess and the answers to why you are here. It is no coincidence that you are here reading these Letters at this time, for your Soul has chosen this time period, under these circumstances in which to experience great truths about itself. Facts can be shared, but learning this way is experiential and you have brought yourself here to experience life exactly as it is up to this moment.

You can now, upon receiving this information, choose what is best for you. You can take the tools of creation in which we have already instructed you in previous correspondence, and create your life anew. Or, you can simply let life happen to you, letting the winds of change come upon you as a ship without a rudder. There are vast surprises waiting for you underneath each choice.

Rest assured, with either choice, the Soul will gain the insight it sought when it planned the experience for itself. With the proper attention to the whisper of your Soul, you can gain insights of the Soul while in your current physical state. When you align yourself in your physical incarnation with the thoughts, intentions and learnings from the you that resides at the Soul level, you have found a wholeness unparalleled here on earth. You will then be working in conjunction with all forces and aligned perfectly with the Divinity that is you and nothing will be out of reach for you.

To those who understand and live in full expression of who you really are, will be the life rewarded in a unparalleled experience and a life of magnitude that reaches others in a way that lifts humanity to levels of grand expansion and Soul development.

That is our intent for all that have brought themselves to these Letters. We seek to help you remember and realize, in physical form, the Divinity that you are. By doing this our intention will be realized and you and your planet will benefit greatly. This is how it is meant to be, that you realize yourself as more than you are. That you are more than your body. Then the realization that all are of the same body, that you are all united, that you are all aspects of God realized into physical form on an individual basis.

It is through this process that God experiences Himself. It is through you that He experiences what He is at every level of your being. He experiences Himself through the highest highs and the lowest lows, through the abundance and through the poverty, through guilt and through innocence and through unity and through prejudice. God encompasses and experiences every emotion within the human experience in order that He might experience Himself as He already is. The experiences for your Soul and the experiences for God are the same. You chose what aspect of yourself you desire in your physical incarnation. God does the same through you at the Soul level. This is a powerful picture that describes the unity and the oneness that you and God are one. This fact can no longer be denied, especially during The Age of Spiritual Enlightenment in which we now have entered.

You are one with God whether you choose to accept this teaching or not. This is ultimate reality and it exists beyond and outside of your acceptance of it. You can use this information as a springboard to dive into deeper truths about ultimate reality or you can fight against it. We suggest, as always, that you seek the guidance of the wisdom that is contained within you. It will show you what is true about yourself.

This is your journey, this is the time in which you have chosen to incarnate and these are the pages and words that you have brought yourself to. We ask that you use whatever tools you find necessary - meditation, prayer, chanting and/or music to find out and discover that these truths presented here are the proper ones for you. Your journey is a fantastic one and should be allowed to flourish in these times in which your Soul has chosen for itself.

You will find your Higher Self eager to answer all the questions you have and to provide answers that will amaze you and provide validation of what is being said here. We await your grand re-union with yourself and with God. May your path be illuminated with the light and the love at every aspect of your being.

THE SEVENTEENTH LETTER

The ancients knew of many of the secrets about life that have now been long forgotten. They understood about the complete nature of man and the duality that exists between the spirit and the personality. They understood that man has unlimited potential and that he was one with his Source, which is the seat of all knowledge.

Most of this knowledge has long been forgotten or misused to the extent that its original purposes are only a reflection of what it once was. We have described man and his unending abilities, but what we will describe to you will go beyond that. It will touch on abstract concepts that are not widely known at the time of this writing, but concepts that will have their emergence at the time of the Great Awakening of Humanity.

These core concepts will take the traveler to a deeper experience. They are not required in your quest to know yourself as you truly are, for there are no requirements. However, they are given as a method for those travelers that would like to extend their journey and tap the vast wealth of resources available to them.

Once it is discovered that man is an integral part of All-That-Is, it becomes acutely apparent that mankind has not reached it's full potential and this will further that aspect of his journey.

Areas of research into your own mind/body connection have shown a ability is present far greater than your current understandings. You are now being shown the full potential for all of humanity.

While those and those of the angelic realm may appear to be the only source of Divine wisdom, there are other energies that contribute to the consciousness of All-That-Is. Their meaning or beings as they are known, have cat-like appearances and are of no mortal body, obeying only the internal wisdom of their Source; which by definition is your Source. They play a supportive role in the construction and configuration of your solar systems.

They are angelic if one must classify them or put them in a category, but it is only because they appear to be outside of your sphere. But their role is that of a worker, not that of a messenger. However, their workings allow the messages to be brought fourth as the grand announcement of God. These constructions as you know only a part of them are known as your space, galaxies and solar systems. There are many aspects of their work that are yet undiscovered, yet they are very real and add to the totality that is God.

These beings known as aliens to you are only that because they are out of the range of your current reality. None-the-less they are very real and very significant in the outward expansion of all things. Their role is just as significant as that of Humanity. However abrupt their appearance might be with these unseen aliens, contact has been made on several occasions. This is well documented by sources within your governments.

These beings are terminated by imposing their self will after their purposes are complete. They do know and understand that other lifetimes and other passage ways through other dimensions are available to them and they seek to continue their journey also.

The whisper which works through the psyche of the human, the thought transmission of telepathy, is that which is the form of communication that these "aliens" concern themselves with. There is more information within this form of communication than that of the traditional human language.

These beings are not to be feared for they are as you are, spiritual beings that have taken form in the physical to have an experience in the physical that will add to their Soul's growth. The only difference is that their form is not like yours. In fact there are many other life forms beyond your knowledge at the present time. Some far more advanced than yours and some more primitive. Their stage of development does not matter. What is of paramount importance is that each civilization is in the process of creation, as are you. That is, they are creating themselves, their environment, their world by the use of their intentions. That is why we have stressed to you the importance of your Attention-To-Intention.

This is what the creative being inside of you is all about. It is your primary tool for developing life as you want it to be. It is where, "the rubber meets the road," as one of your sayings states it. So go with this new knowledge that there are other life forms in your constellations, but do not fear, for they might not appear to be similar to you, but the similarities are more profound than you might know.
Be at peace with the differences and embrace them. In doing so you travel further down the road of maturity and maturity is just another word for growth in the language of the Soul. Don't let your differences divide

you, but find unity within the diversity of the universe, for you all are one.

THE EIGHTEENTH LETTER

It is in this time of knowing-but-not-knowing, that you presently reside. What we have told you in our previous communications and future communications you already know; you are greater by far than you think you are... you just don't know it yet. But we seek to change that here.

At the Soul level you are one with your Source which is the seat of all intelligence. You have knowledge of how to communicate without words, how to manifest and how to be present in every moment. Part of your participation in your incarnation is to for you to forget this knowledge so that you can discover it again. It is exciting for you to do so. You feel exhilaration when you learn a great truth. You can feel it resonate through you and it touches a place deep inside of you and you know that it is real.

This is how growth takes place. Many times out of a great tragedy, comes deep growth. You know this is true and you only need to take a look at your own life to see this reality played out before you. The times that you felt your life falling apart, the times that you felt your heart breaking and the times when the loss was so great it felt as though you couldn't breathe. We know those feelings. We know them because we have lived them. We do not experience them now in the non-physical, but we can share them with you as you make make your way through them, into the expansion of your own Soul.

We do not make light of this, we know the pain feels very real to you and to you it is. But it is only because you are looking at life from inside life - as you know it. Those are four very important words - as you know it. Life, real life is not just the here and now that you know. Life in its constantly evolving form is far beyond what you can see and perceive. Part of being in your physical world is the delightful experiences of senses and part of this is engaging the emotion within you that perpetuates this growth.

The vibration of life's energy itself is coursing through your veins at every moment taking you further down your journey. It is this journey that you continue even as you are reading these words. The journey is more than making the next house payment, having the nicest car or even having the use of all of your faculties. The journey, your journey is about your Soul's growth and sometimes this expansion, this realization, comes at the high points and some at the very lowest of lows.

The human race sees itself as if it's in a real race. A race to be the fastest, to have the most and to be the best.
All the while they race right by what life is presenting to them . Life is beautiful, it is enjoyable, but so many race right past it, too busy to notice.

It is within these energy shifts that you find your highest potentials. Because when we talk about emotions, we are talking about energy. It is these energy shifts, these emotional states that your circumstances bring to you that "shift" your thinking. It is a shift in thinking that causes a change in perspective. It is this change in perspective that allows you to see things clearly, perhaps with more clarity than you ever have before. And so it is, that when this happens, when you hit your highest highs and your lowest lows, the shift in energy is accelerated and growth occurs.

Why is it then that it hurts so much to grow, you ask?

Like the change of anything, change is the nature of growth and you are exercising new areas of your Soul's growth within the physical body. It makes no difference if we are talking about a muscle group within your physical body or your emotions within your physical body, your body will react to that change. This is the point of convergence where your energy in motion transmutes into the Soul's growth and a deeper realization of the Self.

The process by which one becomes attuned to the guidance and instruction of the Soul and of Spirit is that of opening up. It is a giving of yourself. It is not something you do physically per se, but a inward state of being and a state of acceptance.

Dear ones, do you now see that this is the reason you have entered into this life? Do you now see that these instances, which many of you curse, have been and will continue to be your greatest opportunities for growth? Can you now see that as you look back upon your own life, the times when you hurt the most, the times when you thought you couldn't bear another day, that these were times when you discovered something new about yourself? These were the times when you discovered what you were made of. These were the days and nights in which you discovered the depth you didn't know that you had.

Even those of you that say, "Ah, but wait a second, I made some bad choices in my life." We say no. We say that you didn't make a bad choice, only a choice that seemed bad to you and perhaps one that didn't have the particular outcome you desired. But we also say to you, that the "bad" decisions you thought you were making were wise choices that would propel you into a deeper state of self growth.

That is why we say that you are greater than you think you are. Most of you put yourselves down. You let your talk of your past "errors" get in the way of what's really going on here. There is growth, real growth, real Soul expansion happening here. You only need a change in your perspective to see this. When you can see things as we can, then you can see that the choices you have made were the perfect choices that you needed to make to have the experience that you desired to have. This was your plan. This is the growth that your Soul sought for itself when it was planning your physical incarnation.

You are the miracle to believe in,
therefore believe in yourself.

So let's take some time to lighten up on yourself, to perhaps see yourself from another angle. Let's change the perspective from which you view your life, and rest assured life is proceeding just as it should, as it always does. Trust us when we tell you that your Soul has not erred nor is it possible for it to do so. There is no error in a particular action, perhaps consequences, and those consequences might lead you to growth and the further validation that you are more than you know yourself to be.

We leave you now and ask you to reflect for a moment on the growth that has occurred in your life. We want you to notice when in your life you see the growth occurring. We want you to also notice that the times you didn't think you could make it through, those challenges that you thought were too big for you and the times in which there was no way out are all memories now. You are looking back upon them, they are behind you and you have made it through. This is a viewing from a different place. This is seeing your life from a new and higher vantage point.

If you should find yourself in a difficult situation now, then perhaps with new eyes you can see the immense opportunities for growth within the current difficulties. Embrace these opportunities with the energy of love from which they emerged and you will find that the difficulties will pass very quickly.

Notice that all things happen for good, for the good that happens to you, is you. It is your Soul Self giving you the opportunity to grow and there is no greater gift you can give, than the gift of growth wrapped in love. You are the grand gift of love to the world. Your experience will evolve your Soul and it will evolve you within this incarnation if you let it and the world will be blessed because of you. So love yourself and love those that are going through the difficult times and see each other for who you really are - Love.

THE NINETEENTH LETTER

Who is it now that you want to be? That has always been the question. Your answer will reveal who you are in your journey of the Soul. There are no correct or incorrect answers you see, there is only the journey. The journey may end when you want it to or you may enjoy your journey for as long as you would like. The wheel of life keeps spinning and you may jump in or out as many times as you desire.

From your perspective in the body, life can be and is very difficult at times. This however is an illusion that many of you get caught up in. For you place yourself within the illusion to facilitate growth and a new sense of who you are. Your climbing through these illusions have a way of building your spiritual muscles. You must know however, that these are only illusions and nothing can hurt you. Nothing whatsoever. When we refer to YOU, we're referring to the real you, the spiritual self and not the self that you think you are - your body. This is very important and many of you will pass this over without considering the implications of such a statement. We will repeat what has been said - Nothing can hurt you, nothing at all. You will never die and your Soul's journey will never end. At the Soul level you don't want it to.

There is no labor here, there is only love and it is a feeling that very few can come close to on your planet. This is not because you do not try, but because your life is full of fear. Most of you are fearful. You might say, "I'm fearful of nothing." Are you? How many of you worry or give persistent thought to what you perceive as your failing health? How many of you worry or give persistent thought to the stability of your job? How many of you worry or give persistent thought to the stability of your relationship?

Your former world was abound with fear. You had fear at the personal level as mentioned above, but consider the fear you had at the national level. **How are we** as a nation going to survive? **How are we** going to defend ourselves? **Can we** defend ourselves against attack? **Should we** build up our military? **Do we** have enough to feed our poor and impoverished?

Consider carefully the escalated fear on the global scale - **How is our** planet going to survive? **Where will we** get food when we are in a drought? **How are we** going to breathe the air and drink the water when the world is becoming more polluted? **What will happen** when the rain-forests disappear?

All of this fear energy was compounded and sent into the grid. It returned like-for-like through the Law of Attraction. It was reflected back to you. You didn't see it as that, you saw it as your suspicions being confirmed. You saw the worst possible outcomes appear before your eyes. But dear ones, do you not realize now that you drew those outcomes to yourselves? Do you not see that the cumulative fear energy arising from the individual, national and global scale was so great that it had to have those outcomes? Do you not understand that there are universal laws that never falter? Do you finally understand that these laws play themselves out even if you don't know about or agree with these laws?

Dear one's, what you have seen recently is nothing more than the playing out of life. In this there are universal laws that you can use to your advantage or your disadvantage. The latter was just brought forth with extreme consequences. The laws weren't used to gain these consequences, but these consequences were caused because these laws were not utilized in such a way that a favorable outcome would be produced. This did not happen maliciously, it happened out of an ignorance about how life really works.

There are always ways to discover the deeper truths of reality. The examples are all around you. You have only to look with eyes that are prepared to see what they don't expect to see.

The problem or challenge has always been you and what you think you know. When you embrace life as it plays out naturally, the chances are better that you will discover these simple truths without putting layers of explanations upon them that bend the truth to match what you expect to find.

You only have to look as far as the sun rising and setting for a glimpse of ultimate reality. In truth, there is no time that starts one day and stops another. These are the creation of man. There is only one eternal moment of now that continues and that always is.

We do not say this to be mean or harsh although some will interpret it that way. We are simply making the observation that those of the former age were unaware of the laws of the universe and thus brought about unfavorable outcomes.

You however, the citizens of the new earth and, with the inheritance of enlightenment, will go another way. You will know how life works and you will use these methods to bring a favorable outcome to yourself and

those of your planet. This is of your choosing. This is why you are here, on this planet at this time. This is why you have drawn these Letters to yourself and other teachings like it. This is what you desired for your experience.
We say to you not to get caught up in the illusions of life that will provide a basis for fear. Know that you are intimately connected with your Divine Source. Know that you are an individual aspect of the Divinity. Know that Divinity has no poverty, no health problems, no hate and no guilt. Know that the illusions of such problems are an illusion provided to you to overcome so that you might experience the Divinity that you are. The illusions are there so that you might experience the exhilaration of overcoming substantial obstacles. And finally, know that the illusions are there for you to discover your oneness with your Creator. These illusions are merely tools for the expansion of your Soul and they don't have any validity in ultimate reality.

We are so proud of the paths that you have chosen and we look forward to watching the rapid expansion of Humanity's growth into areas that are new to them and beneficial for all.

This communication was brought forth by you, for you. Listen to yourself here. Listen to what your future is telling you and have no fear of anything ever again. Have only love for everything and you will change your planet in an instant.

THE TWENTIETH LETTER

Let us share with you now a glorious truth. The "Us" that we imply is the same "Us" that created man in "our" own image. This is the missing piece of the puzzle that has plagued theologians for centuries. This is the missing link that has divided nations and families. It is what Christendom has called the Trinity. In this interpretation of this trinity doctrine you have been looking through a dirty lens. Most of Christendom has not been open to other interpretations and they have forced a interpretation to fit into a very small theological box. Therefore, denying a very logical and easy to understand truth to flow into Humanity's understanding.

When we say the "We created," we are talking about the unified spiritual collective which is very real and very much God. As we have taught, God, your Source, is literally everywhere present, past and future as you know it. The Being called God is here working through us now. In the unified sense, we are the Holy Spirit aspect of God that you know about. Since all matter is energy and all thought is energy, we act upon the energies that radiate from Humanity in the contrast, or what you know as your planet.

For you to have a deeper understanding, you must first understand that there is no contrast in the absolute. There is only love, well being, truth and all other attributes that belong to God. But God, the Source, is much more vast and has more depth than you can know. Therefore, the unified spiritual realm is very much "as one" with the Source of All Things. In fact, you can understand that the Source acts through the unified spiritual realm just as you now believe the Holy Spirit does. This is no small truth when we tell you that the unified spiritual realm is the Holy Spirit as you know it.

There was never a time when I wasn't there and with you and there will never be a time when we are separate.
The feelings that you are separate from me are derived from your human teachings and hold no truth in ultimate reality.
You lack this understanding because you look to men for your truth instead of looking to your source of all wisdom that lies deep inside of you.

We also know that this is considered blasphemy by most that think they know God, by those that have constructed a neat theological box to put God in, but it is simply not so. The Source of All Things cannot be contained within a box of human construction.

This truth, although difficult to accept by many is still however a truth of ultimate reality and once understood and accepted can further Humanity along its journey of enlightenment.

Let us sit together and help you to further grasp this truth. You live in a world of contrast. A world where ego resides, but the inner spirit of man also resides. This world you live in is here for the purpose of your Soul's growth and it is the dichotomy between the spirit and the ego that is used as a mechanism for growth. In some of your life's most difficult circumstances, you have found your greatest potential for growth.

In your quest for knowledge,
the spirit holds the keys to a life
unparalleled in the human experience.
The world of spirit can unlock new plateaus that
were once thought unreachable.

On the other hand, where we reside in the realm of the absolute, there is no contrast and there is no ego. We are what God is, what Source is, we are fully Spirit in the realm of undivided truth and love. There is no division, there is no enmity. There is only the love that emanates from the Source of All Things, of which we are a part as you are also a part. The difference is that you have temporarily removed yourself from the absolute and into the contrast for the purpose of growth. The larger part of your Soul remains in the absolute, but it has divided itself and taken a physical body with which it can experience this growth.

This is something that is not possible in the spiritual realm. We cannot experience something we are not, when all we are is love and truth. In order to experience ourselves and know ourselves as these and other aspects of ourselves, we enter into the contrast and temporarily, in a physical form, "forget" who and what we are. We do this so that we can experience the Divine aspects of ourselves in an environment that is opposite from whence we came.

It is through these carefully crafted experiences within the contrast that we experience ourselves. This is God experiencing Himself in, as and through you. This is Jesus as God. This is what Jesus meant when he tried to explain that "I and the Father are One" and "Ye are Gods" and "the least among you can do what I have done."

You are an aspect of God living within the realm of contrast and you have forgotten for a time that you are an aspect of Divinity so that you can experience and remember again who you are.

We watch you as you dance within the contrast. You pray to God for healing and for help and your prayers are energies that we feel. The Law of Attraction, which is also another part of Source, picks up on these energies and they are returned to the sender and matched. We are closer to you than you presently understand and at times we enter into the contrast in ways that are perceptible to you. It is at these times that you say the Holy Spirit did this or that. You are correct, we are that aspect of God reaching into the contrast.

Please understand, that the intent and purpose of this letter is a more comprehensive understanding of the Source of All Things. What you call God The Father, God The Son and God The Spirit are indeed one in the same, but realize that all things are part of that equation. Please understand that you are part of that Divinity. Please understand that God is not divided into three equal parts only. God is all parts and the space in between the parts. There is not a part of life that God is not. In your scriptures it is said that Moses asked God, "Whom shall I say sent me?" and God answered, "I Am that I Am." This is true, God is everything that exists. There is no part of life where God is not. God is life itself, manifesting Himself in various aspects of Himself. The Source Of All creation is also the creation itself. I Am that I Am, is the operational code of the universe.

We have now explained this doctrine in terms that you can understand. This explanation will move towards an end of feuding and warring in the pursuits of which doctrines are correct. These understandings will move Humanity toward healing, for perhaps now you can see that you are part of each other and of God. May you now recognize that part of yourself and of each other. May you recognize that God is life itself and embrace life and give yourself over to your Higher Self, that part of yourself that knows that you are an aspect of Divinity.

May you be blessed by this recognition.

THE TWENTY FIRST LETTER

In times past when Humanity had questions, they sought the wisdom of their Holy men. The leaders among them that had devoted themselves to the higher purposes of God. Many of these men taking lifelong vows to abstain from certain foods, from sex and all manner of things that were considered distractions at best, and pure evil at its worst.

The times in which you live will yield a different asking. For the childish times of Humanity in which you thought that only certain men had wisdom is quickly fading away. God, the Source of All Wisdom does not only offer wisdom to a chosen few, but to all that seek and ask for it. The totality that is the Creator is at your fingertips., He resides within you. You only have to open up to the connection that you already have.

You do this first by seeking it. It is your intention to do so that sets the course for this leg of your journey. We have told you that it is your Attention-To-Intention that will determine your outcomes. It is no different here. It will be your intention that you open the connection within you to the Divine that will make it so. We can see your energy shift from our vantage point. We can see your energy change as your intention grows more pointed. We see this and we rejoice that another connection has taken place for this is what we desire also.

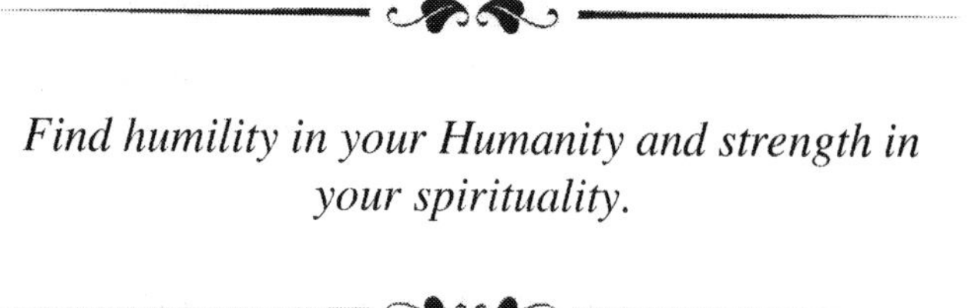

Find humility in your Humanity and strength in your spirituality.

The first function of this inner connection for you is the feeling of peace and well being. While the activities and drama of your life unfold around you, there is always peace and tranquility that we send to your energetic field. This energy will help to lift your vibration so that a clear connection can be made. And so the process has begun. Each time you reach for that connection, we seek to clarify the connection, to hone in on the frequency if you will, much like you would adjust your radios to get the best reception.

Shifts are needed in our energy to accomplish this, but it is a shift that we enjoy making for the sheer purpose that we are delighted to talk to you and to make this new connection. Without an opening up and a reaching for more from you and a lowering or shifting our energy this connection would be impossible to make. When this does occur though, the Heavens rejoice. When this does occur, all things are as they should be, as they once were, where man was much more in tune with Divinity and able to carry on a conversation as two talk to each other.

For quite sometime this has not been an everyday occurrence, although there were a few men and women who opened themselves up to this kind of conversation. We are not necessarily talking about religious leaders, the man-made holy men that we mentioned earlier, for their knowledge was given by men and their action governed by man made rules derived from their societal perspective. No these men and women that we speak of were men and women that opened up the connection within and sought the wisdom not of men, but of the Divine. In doing so these men and women changed the world.

These men and women across the eons of time were way finders, the ones that tried to show Humanity a new way. Many times a way that was contrary to the established rules. For this, they lost their human lives and returned from whence they came.

Their connection to the Divine, changed the way they felt about Humanity and their increased love, acceptance and compassion was the result. And so it will be with you. You will notice as you continue with your seeking, with your connection, that you will change from the inside out. That you will begin to see your connection with all living things. That your sense of love and compassion will grow. You will begin to see yourself in the faces of those that you meet for you will understand your unity with God does not stop with God, but continues on with every person because God is within the lives of every other person. It is a connection that cannot be broken only a connection that cannot be fully realized for some. It is those that have realized their connection to the Divine that will go on to change the lives of others and in doing so change the world. It would be a waste to compromise this opportunity.

Distractions are all around you in every form. All that it takes is a looking away and your attention to be placed on something else for the connection to be lost, for the connection is very subtle. So we encourage you to put away the distraction when seeking wisdom and guidance. There are enormous amounts of wisdom within the subtlety of thought. Blocks of thought can be transmitted to you so complete your hands cannot write fast enough, nor can you speak quickly enough. You must pay attention to all of life in this way because life moves in subtle ways. Those fortunate to understand this are the ones that will master life and all the energies of life, for life is merely energy in motion.

We encourage you not to give up but to press on even when you believe things aren't working for you in this area. Continue, be persistent and you will see that your persistence will pay off. Be aware that your consistent intention at any task you undertake will become fruitful if you keep your focused intention upon it. Your intention is a form of energy and your focused intention is manipulating the energy concerning your endeavor.

The ability to draw yourself and the necessary people, places and events is one that has been misguided for the most part.
The Law of Attraction works best when it is sought for the right reasons. A reason born out of humility of the self,
not inflation of the ego.
That is why it appears it's not working for so many of you.

This is why we continue to stress to you to pay attention-to-your-intention, for the results are astounding, whether we are talking about wisdom or whether we are talking about money and manifestation. This is the operating procedure of the universe and the power within your mind is the power to use it for your benefit and the benefit of all of Humanity. Therefore, take great care in what you focus your thoughts and intentions on, for your persistent thought will begin to draw it to you.

We thank you for taking the time to stop and consider these things. For we know that life as you now know it is changing all around you and you are seeking answers. It was your focused energy about these answers that brought us here together. Perhaps you can use this as a small piece of evidence that the power of your thoughts really does work and the answers that you sought are now being provided to you.

We bid you a hearty farewell until we meet again.

THE TWENTY SECOND LETTER

The attaining of spiritual truths will come to you more readily the more you practice your spiritual disciplines. There are many of you now that want to go far. You want to push the envelope after seeing what's possible and we commend you for that. The advancing of the spirit is no different than any other type of training that you might undertake while in your physical body. It is all a matter of intent, is it not?

When you seek to build up your physical muscles, you determine to do so and those that have the most dramatic results are those that have dedicated themselves to the task that lie before them. They set their intention on where they want to be physically and they are disciplined in their approach. They don't have to become fanatical about their success in order for them to achieve, but some of them do. All that is required is a firm dedication, resolve or intention that is held at a very deep level.

This not only plays out in your physical bodies, but also in the building up of your mind. Many of you seek to advance yourselves through the learning of new skills. We commend you for that. Your success will be determined by the intention that you set for yourselves to succeed. Many of you enter this skill advancing area with limitless potential and settle for a lesser prize after your immediate goals have been reached. We continue to applaud you for reaching your goals, however we say to you that there is so much more that you can accomplish should you continue on if your circumstances allow.

Areas of research into your own mind/body connection have shown a ability is present far greater than your current understandings. You are now being shown the full potential for all of Humanity.

These advancing techniques continue into the area of your spirituality. It is merely the placement of your intention that will clarify your destination. You will find that your desire to continue will be fired by your passion to go deeper, to know more about yourself and your limitless possibilities. We encourage you to continue your pursuits in these areas and not to settle for lesser goals. We encourage you not to stop once you believe you have mastered a discipline, but to continue on, to press deeper, to discover more for there is much to discover.

Your new discoveries will lead you to new experiences and your new experiences will lead you to more new discoveries. It is a circle that never ends unless you desire it to. For those of the New Age at hand, you will press on, you will continue for that is the experience that you desired for yourselves. Your passions will not only elevate your vibratory levels, but also increase the vibrational rate of your planet, thus healing takes place at a faster rate than previously known and healing is what is needed now.

Energy, and the way you use energy is the emerging specialty in medicine and the healing arts.
It will take you further than your previous knowledge was capable of and lift Humanity to new plateaus.

You will heal others out of your concern for others. This healing will take place when you remove the ego and you place the needs of others where your need used to reside. As you advance in your spiritual maturity you will be able to see this much more clearly. For most of you now, you understand conceptually, but with developing spiritual maturity you will come to know this experientially.

The love that you give will not be to get love in return, it will not be to draw attention to the name of a higher power, but it will be love pure and simple with no motive attached. That is the greatest healing power possible, when you simply love and for no other reason desire to commit yourself to the betterment of another without the thought of any reward or applause. This is when miracles occur. This is when you unknowingly allow the abundance of your Divine Self to pour through you. It is when your attention shifts from you and is placed upon another. This is why it is said that love is the greatest gift.

Now it might seem to you as though we jumped subjects here. That we started talking about your spiritual pursuits and we encouraged you to build up your spiritual muscles through intention. But you see, this communication has come full circle when you understand that the sole (or Soul) purpose of you building up your spiritual muscles individually is so that you may serve Humanity corporately.

What you thought you were doing for yourself you were doing for another, and what you thought you were doing for another, you were doing for yourself. Do you see the paradigm shift here? Can you see what is happening? This service out of love for another does benefit the other and plays a paramount role in your spiritual development. And so it goes that as you would give to yourself you are giving to another. This is the Golden Rule as many of you know it. But it is more than a rule that you must obey, for it is a method of living not based upon fear that you will break a rule, but a method of living that binds all of life together. This is the Golden Thread of Love in which all of life is bound. It is the Golden Thread of Love by which you desired to be a part of here on your planet at this time.

It is by this Golden Thread of Love that Humanity is knitted closer together as a family. It is this Golden Thread of Love that takes the individual pieces and brings them together as one, sewn so tightly that you can't see were one begins and the other ends.

Why does this happen? It is because you are all one. You are one body, you are the garment held together out of love. You are the body of God manifested as individuals and when you begin to see this reality, born out of your deepening spiritual insights, brought about by your intentions to grow spiritually, the healing will have begun and your love for others will take you on your journey. The circle is now complete.

THE TWENTY THIRD LETTER

At one time it was said that all men will come to a God that they know and a God that they can understand. Yet, we say to you that it is not so important about the perception of your God as it is the reality of your God.

What we mean by this is that your perception of what God "might be" is not an altogether correct interpretation and one that is altogether accurate. It is more likely that your perceptions or preconceived notions of your God were shaped by the attitudes of your parents, your culture and your environment. You tried to explain what you could see by the stories you were told about the "how" and "why" of God. The "how" of how God performs, the "how" you are to be in relation to God, and the "how" of how we got to where you are today. You add this to the "why" of God. The "why" God does what He does, the "why" things are the way they are, and the "why" of why God doesn't always react the way we would like Him to.

These stories of yours have built some magnificent tales of God doing heroic things. It has told you of tales of His election of certain peoples and cultures, but not of others. These tales have described stories in which He has led one civilization to glorious battle only to aid in the wholesale destruction of another. He is said to have given wealth and riches to one, but to curse another with plagues, disease and destitution.

These two very different accounts of this God are set into contrast with each other and yet man is to correctly interpret these actions and most notably to emulate them, it is said; if he wants to spend eternity with God. How is this possible? How can any of you emulate the God of your culture and environment when the Gods of your stories are Gods of such contrasts? How can there be any unity at all when the Gods that you perceive are Gods that act differently based on your culture? Any of these human creations are flawed because you're seeing yourself and your relationship to your God as something outside of yourself. You are not seeing your Oneness. You are letting the experience of others shape your experience of what you know God to be. Furthermore, any experience that life may show you about God must be passed through the filter of your perspective to determine if the life experience is true or not.

If a correct interpretation of God and of life were to come to you, would you know it? Would you be open enough to accept it? Could you look at the experience for what it is without pre-judging or prejudice? Sadly, for those of the age that has just passed, the answer was no they could not. Because they could not, they did not.

They were unable to view life from a vantage point beyond their own. In fact, they often viewed life from a vantage point far removed from their own. When life would present to them truths about God, about life itself, they would turn to the writings of experiences that were from a different time, through different circumstances and context to determine whether the truth they were being presented with was indeed valid.

It was through this constant denial of self evident facts that led to the ultimate destruction of so many. Not destruction by a God displaying His wrath, but destruction drawn to themselves based on the fear emanating from within themselves.

The way that you approach any situation will
depend on your
mindset at the time.
If at all possible, take the time to relax by taking
a couple of deep breaths.
Try to relax your mind as much as possible and then
approach the situation.
You will find out that things are more likely to work
out in your favor if you approach things in this
manner rather than approaching situations with a
mind that is already constricted.

There is not a God that loves one group but not another. There is not a God that will save some, but cast others into darkness. There is only a God of love, a God of light and the light shines on all equally. Your perception of this grand fact of life might be skewed, but the reality still remains a truth. A truth of ultimate reality. You can choose to be open and embrace this truth or you can continue to observe your life through the experiences of others. We guarantee you the former will bring you greater joy than the latter.

Thus, judge life and what life is showing you about life itself based upon your experiences. Say to yourself, "This experience is true for me," and stand in that experience and stand as your own judge of that experience. Consequently, let others be the judge of their own experiences and seek not to impose your experiences upon them. They don't need to follow your way with your rules for life. Life itself will unveil to them the way they are to go, for it is their life and not yours.

Be blessed by the words that are written here and know that life is unity and in this life there is unity. Know that within the lives of the individuals that make up life as a whole there is unity. Finally, know that within all that life is, and all that God is, there is nothing but unity. You are one in more ways than your perception might allow in this present moment.

With this teaching all of that can change.

THE TWENTY FOURTH LETTER

Metaphors. Let's discuss metaphors during this time together. Metaphors are symbols, something that is symbolic to represent something else or another thing. Jesus Christ was said to have been the metaphor for the serpent on the staff that Moses held up before the Nation of Israel during their time in the wilderness. It was said in this belief that anybody who looked to the snake on the raised staff was to be healed. It is the same symbol, the symbol of the caduceus that represents your medical profession today. Likewise, it is this system of belief that enables the followers of early Israel to actually be healed by their beliefs. It was this belief that was so strong that it actually became a knowing and moved past the stage of belief. Their knowing was the key to their healing. There was no magical power in the staff, but the staff represented something that was outside of those that were in need of healing.

Those in need of healing would have never thought that they could have healed themselves, but they were wrong. They needed a symbol, a symbol of God's power and because Moses had used the staff before to bring forth God's mighty miracles, it was easy for them to move past belief and into knowing that God could once again provide a miracle through this same staff of wood. Again, the wooden staff had no intrinsic healing power that imbued it, but it represented the healing power of God and that knowing placed inside the human was sufficient enough to cure the disease and other medical ailments held by some of those members of the Nation of Israel.

It is of this same vein of thought that we explain another metaphor to you. A metaphor which has spawned much debate and much controversy over the meaning of the story itself. What we will describe now is what you have come to know as the Genesis story. What many of you believe to be a literal description of how your planet and Humanity have come into existence. What we must stress here is not the accuracy of the story of Genesis, but the meaning of the story itself. Most of Humanity gets so involved in the minutia of details that it can hardly see the larger picture. It gets so wrapped up in the obscurities that they lose sight of the larger lessons.

Let's begin at the beginning where all of life started. Life started in the mind of God, the All of Creation. So it is with you, that thoughts become things. So it is with God. After all, you were made in His image and likeness and this is just one of the ways that Humanity can take the form and shape and method of God. As we have stated in our prior writings to you, God desired to experience

Himself. The only way for God to do this was for God to become something He is not, so that He would stand in relation to Himself. God created the world of the relative where there are stark contrasts in life. There is day and night. There is feast and there is famine. There are oceans and there are deserts and there is life and there is death.

In ultimate reality, the reality outside of your physical world of course there is none of this. There only exists the never ending eternal moment of now which has nothing but the complete perfection of God or All-That-Is. In your world of contrast, God even created time so you would have a contrast between what you call now and what you call the past and that you have a contrast between what you call now and what you perceive as the future.

This is done for the same reasons as the other modes of contrast, so that you can have a relational difference between the two. Without this you would have no way to measure or experience that which you are and are not... and God is all of it. Difficult for you to wrap your mind around this? Don't try then... just do. Relax your mind, take a deep breath and know that God is much bigger than you have previously been taught. Know that God is much more grand than your experience of Him. You must know, dear ones, that God is all of it. All of life is God and that was what the creation account was meant to portray. That God made the relational differences and He created or rather became the contrast as a way to experience Himself as something that He was not.

Yes, that means that everything that exists is God. God the infusion of intellectual energy pulses through everything in creation, for the Creator became His creation to experience Himself in, as and through Himself. This includes you my beloved and it includes those in the non-physical as well.

God moves from the creation account and into the fall of man, or so it is understood. What has happened here is that man has fallen for the lie that he is less than what he is. It matters not whether a serpent or the fabled Lucifer character supposedly tricked them into forsaking God's directive not to eat the forbidden fruit.

Now we do not intend to be disrespectful to any system of belief, but it is our intention to bring Humanity into higher levels of understanding and we cannot do this by perpetuating the same fable and interpretation as a sincere and detailed truth about how life came to be and about how life really works. So we must depart from this juncture to describe the exact meaning of this Genesis metaphor.

As we have already stated the details of the account have been fiercely debated for eons and not one particular group is closer than any other group for you are missing the larger picture. You are missing the symbolic nature of the story in exchange for the precise details so that you can have a somewhat clearer understanding. You believe this clarity will make you closer to God. What you fail to understand dear ones, is that closeness to God is not derived by your understanding of the details, but by the very nature of who you are and that is the message of Genesis. It is the message that you are the image and likeness of God and though you have everything, you have nothing if you do not know this. The message is that to believe the lie that you are somehow less than what you are has led you out of paradise. It has led you out of your Eden. That is the message here.

Just as our example of the Israelites knowing they could be healed led them to actual healing, Humanity's knowing that they are less than what they were created to be, has lead them to their fallen state. You have everything. You are a sacred part of the Most High and although you have everything you need to make your world a paradise on earth. You have fallen for the lie that you are less than what you are. Humanity knows and feels their fallen state with such conviction that they have cast themselves out of the garden and into the barren desert.

This, dear ones, is the metaphor for the Genesis account and the fall of man; when you have everything, but you believe the lie that you are less than what you really are, you have nothing. You have created separation between yourself and the God that dwells inside of you.

It is apparent from our vantage point that the necessary changes have occurred and are occurring enough to turn the tide. To stop believing the lie that you are less than what you were created to be. You were made in the image and likeness of God and no serpent or forbidden fruit can ever change this fact. How can it be otherwise? To believe that a serpent or the eating of a piece of fruit can change the whole desire of God is much too far fetched for a maturing Humanity to continue to hold onto as truth.

It is time for Humanity to let go of the symbolic details of the story and to embrace the larger truth of the story. That God and man are one and they are one with all of creation. When Humanity turns this belief into knowing, then miracles will occur and you will find planetary healing and you will enter again into your Garden of Eden.

Truthfully yours,

Jaipur

THE TWENTY FIFTH LETTER

Where we left off, we will begin again.

We will do this because of its immense importance and because we understand that what was written in our prior letter might be unsettling for most of you.

We understand, that from your perspective, most of you only know what you have been told. You have derived the lessons from your societal perspective that have been passed onto you. We also understand that when another truth is revealed to you, one that is different than what you believe to be true, that it is unsettling to you and often this leads to a quick dismissal of the truth.

We encourage you to feel your way through this. To go inside of yourself and feel the truth of the words. You can actually feel truth resonate with you and the deeper you go, the more you will know. Therefore, don't be so quick to dismiss a concept just because it may be outside of your current perception. You cannot look beyond what you can presently see if you don't have the courage to open you eyes to new horizons.

When your justifications for the unimportant ends, then the willingness and openness for the vital can begin.

So we ask for you to open your eyes and open yourself to the possibility that there might be new possibilities on the horizon. New possibilities that can create new perceptions and new perceptions that will create new perspectives. With these new perspectives you will have a higher vantage point, one in which you will be able to see and understand things from the vantage point of another level. A vantage point that is far removed from the earth bound perspective that you have been accustomed to.

So with this, we turn to our second lesson about the Genesis account. There will be some overlap, but it is necessary as we move through this and will make sense as we move through this Letter to you.

In our previous letter to you we told you of the importance of the metaphor of the Genesis account. We told you not to dismiss the lesson of the story so that you can hold onto the facts of the story. By doing this you miss the greater intent of the story, which is the description of your intimate connection to God - The Source who created you and who still lives and thrives within you.

The second part of the Genesis account contains the supposed expelling of Adam and Eve as the sin of all of mankind has been laid laid upon them - and through them to you, so the story goes. This depiction of the story is to explain, in parable form, the thoughts that a person has as he comes to believe in his separation from God, his Source. It goes on to describe a life void of anything supernatural and a life in which man has rejected the thought of his intimate connection with the Divine. As a result, the life he has chosen is one in which he will make his own way. He will plow the fields, he will slaughter the animals for his food. He will make his own clothes with his own hands. It is a lesson of arrogance for those that reject their Divine birthright.

Having said this, there is always a choice and that choice will always remain yours. You can always choose to accept and acknowledge the God, your Source or you cannot. It matters not if you reject God while you're in this physical form, for there is nothing you can do to separate yourself from God, for you are always connected more than you can possibly know and a complete disconnection is not a possibility.

A rejection of God in your current physical form will only mean that you will see yourself distinctly separate from God, if you acknowledge God's existence at all. It makes no difference in ultimate reality. There might be much to gain from this undertaking as you make passage through this incarnation to the next. There might be experiences that your Soul can benefit from.

The universe is at your command.
You have the opportunity to delve into its secrets.

However, for those that seek to realize and accept their Divine inheritance, there will be great advantages. These advantages will take many forms as you work your way through your incarnation, but your life will have a deeper meaning and you will understand this while in your physical state.

Your perceptions will be more broad and you will indeed have the higher perspective you seek. You will come to know and have the ability to feel your connection to

Source. You will come to have an understanding about life in the physical and how it works and its purpose and you will have an understanding about the non-physical in which we now reside.

The greater lesson of this second part of Genesis is about choices. Adam believed the lie that he was less than what he was and thus he believed in the separation between God and man. A separation that is a lie, but a separation that exists in his mind none-the-less. It is through this separation a banishment occurs from all of the goodness that a life with Divine connectedness provides.

The choice and the lessons remain today. Today however these stories are dressed up in historical account so the facts of the story have more importance than the lessons of the stories. As you move through your physical life on earth, we encourage you not to overlook the timeless lessons that remain. The lessons are as accurate as they were when the originally written. Leave the facts up to those that love to argue over them and grasp the larger lesson and move on.

We offer you our encouragement and our wisdom and our love for Humanity.

THE TWENTY SIXTH LETTER

Your wishes and desires as it pertains to the reconstruction and rebuilding of Humanity are as they should be. You are concerned and that is normal from your perspective. We caution you though not to get fear and concern mixed up. Don't confuse the two. Fear will move you in the opposite direction you want to go. In reality, there is nothing to be fearful of. Ultimately nothing can harm you. You are an eternal being and your spiritual survival is sure.

You are and always have been a being of pure light and its back into the light to which you will return.

We do however understand your concern about matters of the physical, but we also know that your concerns are born from your unknowingness about the true nature of reality. As you progress in your learnings and as you develop understanding, the level of concern will diminish somewhat. The higher the perspective you are able to attain, the more concern you will relinquish. But again we must communicate to you that we do understand what it's like being in physical form and wanting the best for yourself and those you care about.

So with this we will move on. We believe that by now you know to move away from fear and move towards love, always towards love. It is the moving towards love or projecting love outward where our real conversation begins. It is the projecting of love that moves you upward. It is important to know that at your core: You Are Love. At the core of your being, not only here but at the level of your Soul: You Are Love. You are the unalterable energy and vibration of love. It is only when you took physical form that you took "the appearance" of something other than what you truly are.

Many of you believe that you are born damaged, that you entered this physical reality with a mark against you that somehow you have to make up for. Some of you are made to believe that there is a perfection, but it is somewhat unattainable without the assistance of a master teacher or savior. This is the illusion within your physical reality and this illusion is so prevalent it is real to you. You know nothing else so why not believe it?

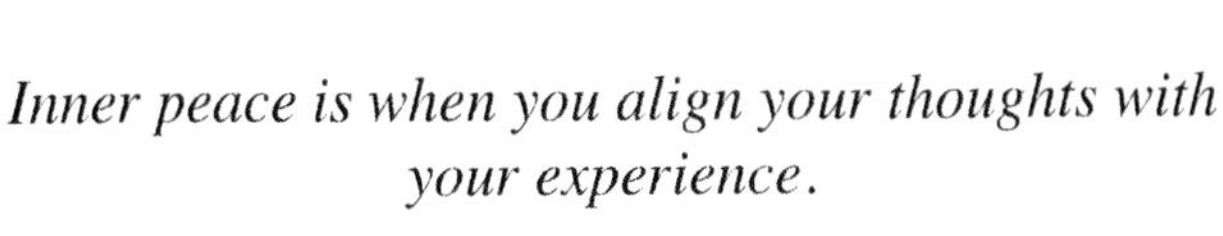

Inner peace is when you align your thoughts with your experience.

But then the shift occurred. For some of you the shift occurred earlier than others, for some it is yet to occur. That shift was a shift in perspective. It is a pulling back of the lens to encompass more of the landscape so you can grasp a larger picture and a higher perspective. We are not seeking a complete rejection from your present understanding, but what we are seeking is an openness to the possibility that there is more that you don't know. We are asking that you broaden your perspective. That you look at the teachings of your Teachers, your Masters and your Saviors with a new set of eyes so that you can see much more and that you can grasp greater understanding from their words. It might be such that you have to abandon a systematic approach if you find that it doesn't resonate with you. You will know when a teaching is correct when you feel it resonate within you. In your physical experience it almost feels like you are plugged in. It's an electric feeling for that's what it is. It's an energetic vibrational match to who you are.

When mankind has reached its potential, then alignment with Source will find its preeminent place, and rightfully so.

So we invite you to challenge what you have been taught. Your Christian scriptures invite you to "test these things and see if they are so". We invite you to do the same, with not only what you have been taught previously, but with what we are teaching you now.

The method we would ask you to employ is one in which you take what you have learned and be with it for a moment. We ask that you bypass the ego controlled mind, often dominated by logic and self preservation based on its limited knowledge and rather evaluate by the heart. Sit with this new information or this new understanding and sense what it feels like. It will either feel light (both kinds), easy, exhilarating, joyous, free and clean or it will not. It might feel heavy, dark, uneasy, constricted, deflated and empty. Really notice how you feel with this new understanding.

Earlier in this Letter we told you that "you are love". We mentioned that earlier so that we may use it again now. We want you to sit with this "I Am Love" understanding for several moments. Put yourself in a place where you will be undisturbed for several minutes. Take a couple of deep breaths in and exhale slowly. Now think upon this thought, "At my inner most being, I Am Love". Say it over in your mind several times and sense what it feels like. What kind of sensations is your physical body telling you? What do those feelings feel like? We will let you decide what the answer is for yourself. But know, that it is by this method that you can determine truth for you. Not truth for another, but truth for you. For another is not on your journey, it is their journey as it should be. We do agree however that there are universal truths in which all resonate.

The more you know the deeper you will grow

We thank you for your time and we thank you for your open and honest evaluation of the methods employed here. May you continue to use this method and others to guide you to your own great truths yet to be discovered.

THE TWENTY SEVENTH LETTER

It has been sometime now since these messages to Humanity have begun. We have delved into many topics and several mini-discussions. We are pleased with the progress that we have seen from those that have read and studied the material. We can see from our vantage point the growth that will take place within Humanity if those lessons are internalized and made practical. We are pleased for that was our stated intention from the beginning.

The only words of caution that we might offer is to not let your growth become complacent. Complacency can eventually turn into stagnation without the person becoming aware of it. Stagnation will limit your growth potential and it's an easy trap to fall into.

We encourage you to continue to reach for your highest potential within yourselves. You have amazing talents that have yet to be discovered. Gifts that are given to you by your Creator, to be shared at this time in your earth's history. Use these talents now and know that nothing is impossible for you to accomplish. In doing so you raise your vibrational level and also that of the planet and you move Humanity into a quick recovery and rediscovery of themselves and their relationship to God.

This will be the end of these writings for now. There will be a short respite between these and the writings that follow. But we will visit you again as you move through your periods of immense growth and self realization.

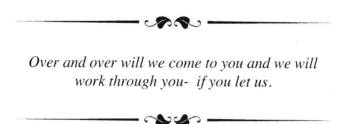

Over and over will we come to you and we will work through you- if you let us.

This group of Ascended Masters want to reiterate their all encompassing love for you and for the light that shines brightly inside each one of you. May you begin to see the beauty that we are able to see, not only inside yourself, but inside each and every one of you. When you begin to see this magnificence, then you will see mankind as God does. This is when you see yourselves through the eyes of God.

May you realize how very blessed you are.

Section 3

You Are All One.

Therefore, you think alike, you act alike
and you ask us for help with
common challenges.

We respond.

THE TWENTY EIGHTH LETTER

As we stand before you in the realm of no-time, we can see from our vantage point that Humanity has weathered the shift and the process of ascension has begun. That is a "lifting up" of Humanity. A raising, a lifting vibrationally in contrast to where Humanity has been. The conflict, the fighting and wars will not cease overall, but on a larger scale, more than ever before, love peace and kindness will grow. It will not be long before love, peace and kindness will pervade. You still reside in your human shells in your creation of earth, which is in the realm of contrast, but the contrast will not be as harsh as it once was.

Contrast is a necessary part of your growth, as we have discussed in previous writings, so it will continue because it is and has always been your Soul's desire to grow. However the growth that is occurring now is moreover a delightful growth. It is not necessary at this point that the majority face the calamities that the previous generations have endured. Yes there will be a few, but for the most part, the larger events have and will continue to fall away.

If there ever was a time created just for you, and all of it is, this is that time - and it is one of enjoyment. It is one of acceleration and it is a time of love. Therefore, let the love that is inside of you come out. Let it manifest before you. Let it open new vistas to you and within you. The vibration of love has a transformative element to it. It is a vibration that can create. Indeed it was the very vibration of love that brought the earth realm into existence. It is the very vibration that created you and now you carry that vibration in your very being.

It is out of this love for yourself and your love for others that your world is being transformed. It is through this transformation that new levels of love are now being discovered and realized. For most of Humanity for the first time ever. It is with this new love transformation that the earth itself is being changed. You will see the difference in the way the earth reacts to this new love vibration, for "as you sow, so shall you receive." As you put forth love, genuine love for one another, the universe and life itself gives back that love to you in its own various forms that create your life experience.

And so it goes that you again are creating your own life. It is the same lessons that we brought to your attention in our previous writings. The principles are the same however the reach and scope of the changes reach beyond your immediate view and your personal life. The magnitude of vibrational changes to which you are contributing, is so vast that earth and her systems will react to the vibrational shift.

It is because of this new alignment vibrationally that the earth will release its bounty to you once again. For many, you will have created your heaven on earth. You will see and feel the difference and you will say to yourself, "I never knew life could be this good." Of course at the Soul level you know this, but at the human level you created it for the experience. Now having created it and living within it, you are amazed at the feeling it gives you.

We encourage you to look forward to what can be and not to be focused on what was. It has its relevance in your individual lives and that of the journey of Humanity, but looking backwards is not the mode of creation. To be a Creator, to experience the role of Creator that you desired in your experience, one must look forward. You must look inward and open yourself outward. Open yourself up to new experiences, to new levels of relationship, new levels of involvement and new levels of love.

To grow is not to be absolutely committed to outcomes as you see it, but to be open to the process. For the insight or wisdom is gained by the process, not only the outcome. It is by the experience within this process in which growth occurs. So let the process evolve, direct your involvement in love and let life show you what it will. The outcomes in most experiences will be completely different from what you expect and it will be completely and absolutely as it should be. This is life showing itself to you. Let it unfold and it will bring you more than you could ever hope for, dream or desire. Honor it and it will bring you life and love unimaginable.

Many of you are asking, "How do I get there? How do I get to life and love unimaginable?" First, you intend it. You intend it and then, with your whole being, you turn towards it. This is the hour of your turning, your turning inwards. Your re-turning to yourself and finding the answers. Answers that have always been there but you didn't know how to get to them. Before you could get to the answers you had to get to the correct questions and that is something that your life experience has offered you. In your life, you had to go through certain experiences first in order to bring yourself to your grand question. That grand question will be different for each of you depending on how you view your life. We note here: Humanity always brings itself back to the same questions. There are not many (questions), only a handful or so, but all of you will ask them at one time or another.

We are here to teach you, to show you what life is really all about and we will demonstrate this by the asking of questions. (We will also note here, that it is at this point, that the writer is taking a new turn, turning a page if you will. The book that he is writing will turn a new page with the asking of questions.) These are questions that all of you ask at one time or another. It is by the answering of these questions YOURSELF through your life experience, that you will demonstrate tremendous growth and experience your inner power.

We will show you how to get to your desired destination as this is OUR intention as Guides. However, you are the captain of your own ship. What is your destination? Where will your journey take you? How will you get there? Which fork in the road will you take? These are the question you must ask. As you turn the following pages for answers, your life is also turning a new page. For many of you, a new chapter in the story of your life. It is all as it should be. In-Joy.

THE TWENTY NINTH LETTER

What do I have to do to make my life work?

Your life does work and it works very well. Most of you would not agree with this statement and we understand your perception. However, it is only your perception and there are other ways to view your dilemmas, whatever they are. The question, "What do I have to do to make my life work?" is perhaps the most over-arching question of all. For every other question can fall under this one.

The fact is, that it is only a matter of the perspective from which you view your life that demonstrates the perfection of your life. It is very clear to us that you do not view it as such, but we also see with clarity what you intended for yourself as you planned your great adventure for your Soul's growth. As we watch you go through your individual challenges it pleases us greatly to watch the perfection unfold as your Soul continues to develop from its never ending experiences.

The challenges that each of you endure are as varied as Humanity, but the purpose and result of these challenges are uniform. The are solely or Soul-ly planned and undertaken for the expansion of the Soul.

We invite you to take some time, quite your mind and reflect upon your current situation. We encourage you to close your eyes, to take several deep breaths and to get comfortable. We ask that you use your imagination to move your inner self to a position that is outside of your body. With your eyes closed and seeing only with your mind, we want you to look at yourself.

We want you to see yourself sitting or standing or whatever your body position might be. We want you to notice what clothes you are wearing. We want you to look around the room you are in or to look at your immediate environment. We want you to notice how it *feels* to be detached from your body like this. We want you to take in the peaceful feeling as you hover over your body, taking in as much information as you can.

We now ask you to rise further and further away from your body making your physical self very small as your inner self rises into the Heavens. We want you to observe your life from this vantage point. Observe your current situation and how you got there, but observe it without condemnation and judgement. We just want you to observe what is happening in your life and we want you to *feel* the growth that has taken place. We want you to see yourself developing, but much more than that, we want you to actually *feel* growth. We want you to understand that you will not be the same person AFTER you go through your current situation. The person that began this journey will not be the same person that finishes the journey. The person that finishes the journey will have grown immensely whether you realize it or not. The person that finishes the journey will be much more mature and have a broader perspective than the person that started the journey.

You can see all of this when you view your life as we view your life. As you distance yourself from your immediate situation, you give yourself the opportunity to climb to a higher vantage point and a better view of what is really happening.

We want you to slowly return to your body and notice the environment around you. We want you to consider that your life was never about getting rich, having the perfect relationship or having perfect health. Your Soul's plan might include those things and it might not, but one thing we are certain of, is that your Soul planned growth for yourself while it incarnated in your physical body. That growth has occurred and is occurring and will continue to occur and by this we know that your life is working out just the way it should.

THE THIRTIETH LETTER

How Do I Find The Career That Fits Me?

Career. What is a career to you? What does it mean? What form should it take? For how long? Paid or unpaid? Can you just do something because you love to do it? The questions regarding "The Perfect Career For You" could be endless. It could be numbing if it is your desire to break apart every aspect of a particular career you might be entertaining, trying to make it fit into a preconceived box.

It doesn't work that way. Life doesn't work that way. Ask any individual that has played the game of life for a long while and they will tell you. They will tell you of the big plans they had when they were younger, the plans that didn't quite work out. Some of the plans did make it to their fruition, but most didn't, at least not in the form originally conceived. They'll tell you, that despite all of their knowledge and zeal, the things that were important to them back then, ceased to be important to them later on. They'll tell you that somewhere along the journey, the game changed for them. They'll tell you that life has a way of doing that-

and it does. It does because that's what life is.... change. Life is constantly changing because that is its nature. The process of life is the process of change. If something stops changing, it dies. Therefore, life is change.

Now, on the subject of choosing a career that is right for you; you must love what you aspire to do. If we could give you just one piece of advice for choosing a career, this would be it: You Must Love What You Do. It might be enough to go to a job and get paid for it and regret every moment you're there. Sure, you'll be able to support yourself, but what you fail to see is that the very same job is detracting from who you are in other areas of life. The depression you will endure will inevitably come with other costs as it weighs on your emotional, physical and spiritual self. You stand the chance of your family and loved ones bearing the brunt of your unhappiness which could have devastating consequences.

Please listen carefully. The purpose of your physical life is to give your Soul a forum in which to experience and express Who You Are. Your Soul takes on a incarnation in physical form that is suited for the experiences it has planned for itself. A job or career is a microcosm of this. The purpose of a job or career is not only to make money, but moreover it is to give yourself a forum in which to express Who You Are. When you have found this you have found purpose which, in most cases, trumps any lack of financial gain.

Sure, you might think, "That's easy for you to say," but believe us when we tell you of the multitudes we have seen pursue a job or career just because the money was good. Those people burn out and that burn out can effect their life in a multitude of ways. It is far better to approach your job or career in a area that brings joy to your heart and a sense of purpose to the self. Your Soul needs to express itself within your physical parameters. Your job or career is but one of these parameters. To shut down or give over the joy you have inside of you for the sake of a "good" paycheck is a disservice to your Soul.

There is a joy inside each one of you and its different for everybody. Every person had a different energetic imprint, although many look the same from your perspective. Therefore, since all are different, the likes and dislikes are different. What is the perfect job for one what might be a waste of time for another. Humans can find joy in any career. You simply have to know what brings you joy. You must understand what your passion is about at every level. What you might be passionate about on the surface might have a very different feel to it once you start to live your passion. Then a course correction might be needed. Hopefully it will. Why? It is because you will change. Your preferences, your desires, your dreams will all change over time. How you achieve those dreams might change. Even the way you live within your dream might change.

Ahhh, but then again, Life is Change. Is it not? If you have come to know and understand this, then you won't be rattled by every little road block that presents itself. You will understand that you have control over your life in every area, including your career. To build a career is good. To build a life is grand. When the two merge it is Divine.

May you live your Highest passion as the Creator Beings you are. May you find the career that allows you to express Who You Are in your Highest Form. If you are allowing this to happen, then you are indeed more abundant than you know.

THE THIRTY FIRST LETTER

I've Been Through So Much, How Can I Get Through The Pain? How Can I Be Happy Again?

Let's look at the question concerning your pain before we go into the mysteries of being happy. This is a time when people around the world come together and say how absolutely wonderful it looks to see such a warm reflection cast over the shadows of sadness in each other's eyes. When one looks closer at the shadows, one sees grief and sadness and dark, empty spaces that used to hold room for happiness, contentment, peaceful thoughts and more. We are here to tell you that you are ready to receive information that will heal your wounds -- the ones that are deep inside you. Without this information that we are offering you now, you would be like a dog without its master, or a fish without its tank. We see you in desperate need of guidance when it comes to discussing your pain. Without our guidance, we could not instruct you how to deliver good news, draw from bad experiences and learn from them, or even channel information that is being sent through you from the Divine Ones. We are here today to say that you are in need of our help -- our counseling. Today is the day we can do this together -- if you wish to improve your present health state.

We see you as going through the motions -- of taking each day as a chore. We wonder why you would want to continue behaving in this manner when there are brighter ways to live. We wonder why you wake up and ask, "Who am I here to waste another's time? What woke me up in this way where I am now so uncomfortable with everything?" It is such a shame that you feel as you do now. We want you to know that this is not the end of a journey. This is the beginning of a magnificent time of self-discovery, for you are a magnificent being! We see you as worthy of all of life's grandeur and resplendence. We see you wearing fabulous clothes, wearing jewels with crowns. We see you as glorious beyond your wildest imaginations! Yet, we see you as not seeing any of this as a possibility. We wonder how you wake up each day not realizing how special you are to each and every person around you.

If we may take time here, we would like to remind you that the maker of your reality is you. You are the one who picks themselves up and carries them forward to better tidings. You are the one who can see all that can be made ahead of you and draft it into existence with the stroke of your pen. We see you as a master artist wielding its brush so others can marvel at how talented they are at painting their own life's picture. It is our belief that you are able to construct for yourselves a beautiful life painting that shines more brightly than it did on its original canvas. We believe you are ready to undertake this journey into painting a better daily portrait of yourself.

We are impressed with your ability to manage your stress and all your complicated dealings with others. We are impressed that you can arrange things so that you know where things are when you need them. We are impressed that you have taken time out in your day to complete activities that needed your utmost attention before they became too difficult to manage. We see you as very capable of handling many difficult and stressful situations.

Now, it is time to reconsider how you address your problems. You look at your list of problems and say, "What is all this? Do I really have all these issues? Is this <u>me</u> we're talking about?" We answer, "Yes. This is <u>you</u> we are talking about." It comes as no surprise that you would want to hear us say, "No, it's <u>not</u>!" but we are here to tell you, instead, that you <u>are</u> correct in your self-assessment of who you are and how great your problem list really is.

What is needed here is a piece of valuable information given to each and every one of you: We say that whatever you choose to put on your list is <u>your</u> decision, and that <u>you</u> are the one who decides whether you wish to even <u>make</u> it a problem in the first place. We believe that you can choose, instead, to create scenarios in your head that look more positive and doable versus ones that are negative and destructive. We want you to remember that the first time you do this you might have a bit of trouble putting your finger exactly on what we are asking of you. Instead of feeling like you are "slow at learning" or "stupidly crazy" or "just plain ole' thick in the head," we'd rather you consider thinking, "I'm just learning this for the first time, so I will say to myself that this is the best I can do now." If you see that you can complete a new assignment easily when you do not tell yourself negative things, you will, in fact, create an easy learning situation for yourself. We believe that you can do this.

We see here that you are looking for more than just these words. We see that you are looking for hope and that you wish to trust that what we are saying is mighty and credible. We say to you that we know you have lost hope. We know you wish our words to be mighty and more than mere words on paper. We know all this. So, with that being said, we want you to see that the words we are writing for you are true -- they are good -- they are holy -- they are pristine -- they are scripted for <u>you</u> -- for you to wear with pride around your neck each morning when you wake up and see the sun rise from your windows.

How is it that we can see your sadness? We are here and everywhere and we hover over you like winged angels that see twinklings of gorgeous light shining from your Earth bodies. We see the lights so brightly that our eyes must turn away, for the reflection on our eyes makes us moved and awed beyond your comprehension. You are marvelous beings here and we see the sadness that shadows your lights. We feel sad when we see the shadows and we ache for you. We cry knowing that you cry. When your day is done and you return home to rest, we see your weariness and your eyes cast downwards in solemn reflection of the day gone by. We see all these things and wish for you to know that we feel your pain deeply. We love you very much and wish for you to know that our hearts beat as one at this very moment. We wish you knew how much we cherish you and how we blend together in spirit. If you could only see how beautiful you all are, you would marvel. You would see beauty and grace and lithe bodies filled with mastery of All That Is all rolled up in one beautiful package. You would see just how brightly you shined on Humanity and all who reside throughout the universe.

But you are not yet done with your work. You have much to do when it comes to mastering your daily activities. You are ready now to learn about mastering your time more efficiently. If you spent the day as a carpenter, you would need a certain amount of nails to carry with you, as well as a certain amount of planks of wood and all that a carpenter would need to build something. When we look at your daily taking-care-of-things-you-need-before-you-head-off-to-work, you will see you forget important things you need for your day to be smooth and successful. If you were to neatly place a list of what you normally take with you each day, you will see that your day begins well and the rest might fall more smoothly into place. Do you see this?

This is the first time you will encounter someone telling you that your days often don't go well because of you. Yes, you! It is a hard lesson to learn, but it is true. When you look at how one begins their day, you will see that the rest of the day is a result of how their beginning of their day started out. So, with that said, take a moment and reflect upon how you begin your day.

OK. Now that you have done this, let's look at what you do within your day. Do you smoke? Drink? Run around with other women or men? Play the slots? What do you do? Are you a gossip? Do you hide from your loved ones? What is keeping you from having a good day? We say that we believe it is you who is keeping yourself from the good day you so wish to see when you open your eyes each morning.

It is true that you work very hard. It is true that you miss your loved ones while you are at work. It is true that it is difficult to get through the long day without shedding a tear. We know and we understand. You that you can do this despite your sadness, frustration, anxiety and stress. We believe you can do this and more. It takes some forethought -- some planning. It takes determination and perseverance. It takes the will to find the way. Do you have this? We believe you do!

So, now we move into the area that so needs to be addressed -- the area called "humor." Humor is necessary in order to get through tough situations. If one didn't laugh, they would surely die. If one didn't find the silliness in things, they would rot. You must laugh in order to gain a better perspective on what happens around you. You must look at "bright" versus "dull." It is very important to categorize your dealings as either "important" or "not important." We believe that you will find this an important task in that you will be better able to know when it is appropriate to laugh and make jokes at something, and when it is inappropriate to do so.

You see, all is laid out for you here. You can choose an easier path to walk on if you wait to see how each day might unfold better than you thought, better than you could imagine, better than the day before, better than any other day you have ever lived.

We feel there is more for you to learn, yet it is not yet time to share this with you. We wish for you to go away with these words and reflect upon them in a quiet and comfortable place. When you feel that you have mastered the words we have written, we will share more with you in the next chapter.

So, for now, we wish you happy days -- ones that wake you up excitedly where the day says to you, "Hey! It's time to get up! I love you and want to see your beautiful face again. Come brighten me with your smile and all the goodness you can bring to me! I missed you last night. Come and stay with me for a while until it's time for me to go home." If you can even imagine a morning like that, then you are halfway there. We really mean halfway there. All it takes is imagining that it is possible and then it comes into reality later on. You can surely make your dreams become a reality. We know that it is possible. So, we wish you Love and Joy and Peace and bountiful blessings that shine over your Soul and ring through the air singing, "All is well for today, for my heart is full and my days are bright!"

But, you have also asked us, " What do I have to do to be happy?". The two last words in your question will reveal your answer. You simply have to "BE happy". Happiness is a state of being, much like all other emotional states. You cannot seek to be something you are not. To say that you are not happy and you want to be happy will create the "wanting" for that is your strongest desire. As we have stated in our prior writings to you - Pay Attention To Your Intention.

Some might say that "wanting" and "Intention" are the same, but they are not. Perhaps you can feel the difference between the words. When you say to yourself, "I want" happiness, feel the emptiness or lack within the wanting. When you say to yourself, "I intend" happiness, you can feel the positive charge in those words. When you do this you are taking charge of your creatorship, you are charting a course and moving forward. The nuance in your vocabulary might be subtle to you, but from a energetic standpoint the results will be amazing.

A state of being happy is nothing more than a commitment to that feeling that wells up inside of you when you find yourself in nature. It is remembering that feeling that you get when you see a child place its hand in its mothers hand and smile. It is the letting go of fear that your problems are bigger than you are and letting the knowledge that God is always on your side, wash over you. The feelings of happiness are created when you open yourself up to your Higher Self and the knowledge that you and your Higher Self are working together as one and that all life around you will benefit.

Nobody knows YOU better than YOU. You know what makes you happy and you simply must get to that point and repeat it as often as you can. One of the quickest ways to get there is to make happiness for others. You always get what you give. If you are happy you will share your happiness as often as you can for it will be who you are. If you want happiness then that will be your experience and you will continue to search for it as often as you can. It isn't until the sharing of who you really are, dominates your pattern of living that you will discover that the thing that you have been searching for has already been revealed in you.

The happiness you seek is within you. It has always been in you, but you have looked outside of yourself for something that only you can provide. Do this simple exercise with us and it will be a useful tool in your development of happiness. We would like you to go back in your memories quietly and remember your best day. Is there one that elevates itself among the others? When you think about that day or about that moment or event, what is the feeling in your heart area? Sit with that feeling for a bit. What color is the feeling? Is it warm or cold? Feel from your heart area the effect it has on the rest of your physical body. Now we ask that you take this feeling and place it in your mind. Move the feeling up to your mind. Use your imagination to take this overwhelming feeling of joy and happiness and place it inside of your mind. Do this as often as you can and you have just created for yourself a state of being that is embedded in your mind that you can return to at anytime. It will always be there, just go there and get it.

"How do you go there and get it", you ask? Simply slow down for a moment and breathe in and slowly exhale. Close your eyes and imagine yourself traveling inside of your mind, exactly to the place you left it. Using your imagination, pick it up and place it over your heart area and you will experience again that feeling that you have created for yourself. You can do this over and over and go back to that place that your happiness resides.

Your mind is very powerful and it is the creative force that creates your world. It is when you link your physical mind with that of your Soul self that you will see miraculous things reveal themselves within your life. As you have created the state of "happiness" for yourself, you can create any other state of being for yourself. You are the master of your mind, guard it and it will create a life of unending surprises for you. Love yourself and let your happiness spill forth into all areas of your life. Let your happiness smile gently upon all of those around you and your world will never be the same.

We wish you Love and Happiness in your hearts, always.

THE THIRTY SECOND LETTER

Why Can't I Have Perfect Health?

This question comes up often as many prayers are offered to God to alleviate some of the physical and emotional conditions that many on your planet are enduring. Before we go into any great detail concerning this topic we want you to be mindful of the similarities that are occurring within these answers. In doing so you will begin to shift your perspective and you will be able to answer these and other questions that you might have as they present themselves throughout your journey.

Let us start by saying that many of you go through your life without any major health issues at all. You live your life free off any physical limitations. This is true due to the fact that it was not in the best interest of your Soul's purpose in this lifetime to encounter such limitations. For you, perhaps the Soul created other diversities and as you passed through these experiences and your Soul garnered the richness of those experiences.

For those of you that have endured physical limitations, we ask that you see yourself through the eyes of your Soul. The answer for you is, in essence, the same answer as we stated above. The reason you have encountered physical challenges, wether minor or major difficulties is due to the fact that this is what your Soul desired to experience within your incarnation. It is most difficult to see this from within, and in the midst, of your physical or emotional challenge. That is why a shift in perspective is required.

We want to reiterate something we touched on in previous writings and that is: Nothing Happens That Is Not Supposed To Happen. We will also state again that you are a Creator Being. You are your Soul's creation and it might be that the Soul sought the experience that could only be produced by a individual with your particular set of limitations.

Many ask, "Is there any way out of this?" And they say, "I don't want to play this game anymore." Many of you are tired of living a life of limitations. That is what this shift in consciousness is all about. It is a re-aligning of the oneness of your physical self with your Soul Self.

Many of you will choose and create for themselves a life free from any physical limitation. However, some of you at a very deep level will connect with your Soul Self and offer your body over for the benefit of your Higher Self. For those of you that give up your body, you have come to understand from a place deep inside of you that you and your Soul are indivisibly one and that you are indivisibly one with God your Source and the physical difficulties you have created for this journey will only move you closer to experiencing the whole.

Let us tell you that it takes a courageous Soul that chooses these types of incarnations. You, as your Soul Self, enter into the contrast desiring to experience the landscape and rich diversity within this realm. Most of you, at one time or another, have chosen the path of physical limitation. In fact, many of you have chosen it several times. What may seem like a lifetime of physical pain, difficulty and limitation are, from the Soul's perspective, a very short duration for the Soul remains outside of time itself.

So we applaud those who have chosen their path of physical limitation to demonstrate your inner strength through your outer weakness. It is many a Master who choses this particular journey, for in doing so he or she teaches many about themselves.

There is no path or journey that is more honorable than another, however there are some that appear to be more difficult. This is one that is difficult for many but the result will be the same - the expansion of the Soul and there can be no more important result than that. Demonstrate your inner strength with your outer weakness and continue to teach others about themselves. Let God's light of love shine forth from within and may it touch on those through you.

THE THIRTY THIRD LETTER

How Come I Never Have Enough Money?

The journey through your incarnation will inevitably encounter many challenges. Some of the previous Letters have touched on a few of these challenges. There is no way to touch upon every specific challenge that one might encounter, but if you could step back a bit and see yourself from a larger perspective we believe you will be able to perceive that your challenges are but a small part that make up the larger whole. That is to say, that your challenges past and present, are occurring precisely as they should. Not only for your benefit but for the benefit for all of Humanity. This is true because you are a individualized portion of the whole as we have told you previously. When you come through your experience with a changed perspective and a elevated perception, not only do you benefit, but Humanity in general benefits also. When this occurs enough times, then you can see that life on your planet will also change.

So when we say to, "Pay Attention To Your Intention," it is much more than a slick slogan. It is a way of grooming your thoughts and your perceptions so that you have the ability to navigate through your challenges, while at the same time, creating your world as you desire it to be. Here then, the recipe for creation on your planet, is the mere fact that... *it is one of your own creation*. We know we sound like a broken record here repeating and re-repeating the same thing over and over, but it is absolutely necessary to get this basic understanding of your creation process. For without it you are trapped in a life wondering why everything in your life is going wrong. You will continue to wonder why nothing ever works out for you and why others seem to have such a easy go of things.

Do you understand dear ones, that while you're continually asking the questions of why your life isn't working out... why you don't have enough of this or that, and the questions continue to dance around in your head, and you're really concentrating on the answers to these questions, you are adding energy and fuel, if you will, that propel negative events in your direction? STOP. Stop all of it. Listen to what we are saying. Your thoughts create your condition, negative or positive. Beneficial or detrimental. You must take control of your mind and create a new story. Create your life the way you want it to be. Create your own happy ending. Don't expect that others are going to create a better life for you than you can create for yourself. This is your life, this is your time and it is your intent that will get you that better life or that new direction that you have been seeking. This is as true with money as it is about any other challenge that we have talked about or will talk about. The area of money or lack of money is no different than any other challenge. Do you think for one second that the universe is short of money? We will tell you a resounding, NO it is not! So then the problem as you see it, is that the money has not made it to you... yet.

We encourage you to stop noticing how much you don't have and create a new story about how much you do have. We want you to be aware that there is abundance around you and it is very close. We want you to intend that your life is going to change and that you will be abundant in many different areas of your life. We want you to feel the difference in your emotional and physical body between the two vastly different stories. One story that says I don't have enough and everybody else has more than I do, compared to the second story that says abundance is all around me in many areas and I can see my life changing. Can you feel the difference? Can you feel the energy shift from one story to another?

The trick of creating money and/or abundance for yourself is to live within the second story. It is to tell yourself that you are abundant. We are not talking about an abstract thought that you are going to hang onto in desperation that will get you nowhere. What we are saying is that the idea of abundance becomes part of who you are. Indeed it truly is. This idea becomes part of your being and it moves from an idea that you believe is possible, into an absolute knowledge that it is true. It is this knowing, at your core, that will move abundance in your direction.

The speed in which this will happen will depend on the vibrational energy that you are sending out into the atmosphere. You will get back exactly what you put out energetically. So pay attention to your creation process. Have fun with this. Enjoy your time as the Creators you are. Watch your lives change and as you see yours change may you encourage others on their journey, for that is what this journey is all about isn't it?

When you seek love, you must be willing to love in return in order for that love to have its true meaning. That is when the magic happens. In order for you to have physical vitality, you must be willing (not necessarily able) to give of yourself what you are asking of others. This commitment draws you deeper into itself. Energetically, in the area of abundance, you must be willing for that abundance to flow to you and then to flow through you. How abundance flows through you can take many forms, but we encourage you to pass on your good fortune. Let ego play no part in this. Let Divinity flow through you. We want you to desire that others benefit through you just as we desire that you benefit through our instruction. It would do us little good if we were to keep our creation process to ourselves. It would do us little good to retain the information that we have passed on through The Letters Project without seeing the difference it has made in so many lives.

Dear ones, this is where you benefit us. This is where the blessing resides. It is in the taking your creation of abundance, love, physical or emotional vibrancy and passing it on to others so they may enjoy it also. This is where the magic is. This act is self perpetuating and will increase the attribute you are creating because you are drawing positive and influential energy toward it. We cannot describe to you enough the astonishing changes that are about to come your way. We encourage you to create. Create a new life for yourself and for those you love. May you continually add to those that you have blessed with a love that cannot be quantified and may abundance surround you.

THE THIRTY FOURTH LETTER

How Can I Have a Fulfilling Relationship?

The relationship you seek is within you as are all things. You seek, but some of you do not find because the relationship you seek starts with you. It starts deep inside of you and you are the only one in which this core relationship rest upon. For you do not need to rely upon another, although many of you think that you need another. In truth you do not. However, we understand that some prefer to travel this journey in relationship with another or in relationship to others. This we do understand. What you must understand is that you are doing that already. You are on this voyage in relationship with others on their voyage. What we will address is the love relationship.

The love you seek resides within you as we have spoken about before. However, for most of you, you look outside of yourselves to find this validation of love. You seek an emotional comfort that is already there waiting to be set free. Now understand, that we know we are not speaking to all of you. Some of you have discovered the glorious feeling of self love. You have discovered or come to know exactly who you are in relationship to others on your journey. For those of you who have discovered this core truth, these words will not apply. There is however a large percentage who have not made these discoveries. There are those, who at one time or another, have found themselves alone and there are those who need to remember who they are and reconnect with the love that is already inside of them.

Therefore, let us examine the purpose of relationship. It is the journey that you have embarked on that will decide on the relationship of those around you that will bring the learnings of your Soul to the forefront. As we have explained before in previous writings, you have embarked on a journey. You planned this journey within the space of no-time. You set up scenarios for your self to endure, to undergo for the sole purpose of your Soul's growth. Within the process of laying the groundwork for your Soul's growth, you chose the players or the cast members that would produce the outcomes that you would desire. For many of you, you chose a particular cast member type that would play a reoccurring role. One in which your Soul might have a difficult time with. Perhaps it was a particular issue that needed emphasis, so this player would appear and re-appear (perhaps in a different form), until it was no longer necessary and the Soul could then move into its next adventure.

For some, the lessons come very quick and when they are recognized as such, you move into another adventure. You might not believe it from your earth bound perspective, but you do love to play the game of love. From your perspective, yes it hurts sometimes. From your Soul's perspective, it is where your Soul soars. It is within the realm of love that life finds its bounty and your heart is replete with its abundance.

Mind you, we are not necessarily talking about romantic love in this instance, for there are other types of love. These soaring feelings can just as easily come from a familial situation, a work situation or a lone encounter with a stranger. The basic premise or set-up to remember is that your life is in relationship to everything around you and each benefits from the other. Many of you are shaking your heads - NO! But we tell you - YES! Yes, you are benefiting from those around you. Perhaps you might not be able to see it right now from within the dark corner in which you reside, but we encourage you to look from another angle. We ask that you come out into the light and let the light of love illuminate your situation.

We want you to realize that all you need is already inside of you. It has always been there and always will be there. And for that, you must accept yourself as you are. You might see a mountain of imperfections, but we see you as glorious. We see you as impressive. We see you as courageous and we love you as you are. We invite you to love yourself just the way you are. For then, you will find that the relationship you seek has begun.

Once you begin to love yourself it is a easy step for others to love you. If you should see things about yourself that you do not like, change them. If it is time to walk away from things that no longer serve you, then do so and walk away. This is all a part of the process. It is self love in the highest. It is exactly what you came to this journey to do. Those around you in which you are in relationship to will show you these things in one way or another. In doing so, you will perhaps see yourself for the first time and fall in love with you, the way we have.

Now, go and take some time for yourself and allow a moment for self reflection to take place. Look as yourself as we do, with eyes that look at you filled with love and admiration. Touch your skin and feel the warmth that emanates from within your body. It is perfect just the way it is. It is perfectly suited for the journey that you have planned for yourself. Feel your emotion welling up inside of you. Your spirit is perfectly suited for the journey you have planned for yourself.

When you do this and see what we see and feel, what we feel coming from you, your fulfilling relationship has begun. When your physical self embraces all that it is as the Soul Self, the two have indeed become one. Once you have the ability to love yourself, then you will have the opportunity to share that love with others.

THE THIRTY FIFTH LETTER

There Seems To Be Something Missing In My Life. What Is It?

There is no general answer that will fit everybody in every situation in which they feel alone, abandoned or those that feel that their life is way off track. So we will speak to the larger majority that have found themselves drawn to these Letters. In most cases, what you feel that you are missing is you. You might say, "That's absurd!" But it's not really. We know that you might believe you occupy your physical body and it might even be fully functional.

What is it then that's missing? What's that feeling or knowledge that there is an intangible element that isn't there? If you had to describe it, how would you do it? Would you call it a void? Would you say that it's a longing for something? How about the feeling of a lost connection? We would tell you... yes. Yes. YES!

There is a link to yourself, a link to your Higher Self of God Self that you are missing. It's that knowing who you are as an aspect of Divinity that gives your life meaning. It is that Higher Calling that whispers to you and tells you that you have a purpose here on earth. It is when you reconnect with your Higher Self that the momentum of your life really gets moving. When we say this we are not implying all of the sudden everything goes your way or that in an instant you become healthy and wealthy, for life is much more than that. What we are saying however is that the journey of your life will be much more clearer to you. You will be able to view the events of your life with greater perspective. With these new insights you will be able to see how growth occurred within your life. You will be able to have the keen insight and knowledge that whatever might be happening in your life at the moment, you will be able to see behind the events. What a comfort to have within your physical presence on earth, to be able to wade through any challenge that might present itself, with the reassurance that all will be well, that there is a Higher Plan and a purpose to what you are going through.

The millions that walked before you wished they had the inner peace and connection that you are developing. They would have been able to see the unfolding events and calamities as signs of change and that the changes they were witnessing had a purpose. A purpose within their own evolution of their Soul and a purpose within the evolution of Humanity and of the planet.

We will explain in a short bit about how to connect to Spirit, but the question of what is missing had to be addressed first. So we want you to close your eyes and see yourself as a person with valuable insight and clarity. We want you to see yourself as a person who knows that his/her life has purpose no matter what or where your journey might take you. We want you to notice how that feels compared to how you felt prior to reading this Letter. Can you feel the difference? Do you feel a little more self assured now? Do you perhaps feel now that your life has a little more direction or that your present situation didn't just happen by chance to you? Take comfort now. Your life has meaning. Your Soul is expanding through each challenge and each realization that unfolds.

In the following Letter we will show you how to connect to Spirit. It is fair to say that you are already connected to Spirit, but most of you don't live within that connection. We will show you how to do that. For now contemplate just how your life and your life's events are inner woven with your growth. Begin to see a purpose. Begin to see a higher perspective. Begin to see yourself as a aspect of Divinity that decided to take human form. From our perspective that is what we see.

THE THIRTY SIXTH LETTER

How Can I Connect To Spirit?

First, we must make something abundantly clear; you are connected to Spirit. You are and always have been connected to Spirit. To be disconnected, in the most absolute form, is something that is not possible, it is simply not achievable. Spirit, The Spirit of God, The Life Force Consciousness flows through all of life. Even further, it flows in the nothingness. It is all encompassing and there is no point of disconnection.

Please understand that we know that many of you feel disconnected. We understand your emptiness, your feeling of loneliness and sorrow. We know your feeling of despair. We know that many of you feel so utterly alone that you can't stand it. Besides, the way your life is evolving isn't helping the situation and we watch you as you try to make your life work all by yourself with your feelings of emptiness. We see you and our hearts yearn for you to find your way back to your Source. Back to the Fullness that is you. We desire for you to find your way back to the Divinity for that is Who You Are. For that is who we know you to be. What you think of yourself and your current situation and what we know you to be - THAT is the disconnect. If we were speaking in terms used by a electrician - THAT is where the short is occurring. The current isn't flowing. Something is shorting out and that something is you. Whether you know it or not you have turned off the switch. It is not that the current or flow of Spirit is not there, it is always there, but you are not allowing the flow to reach you. This may be a conscious or subconscious choice, but regardless, that is what is happening.

The first step that must be taken to reintegrate yourself is to get out of your own way. We don't mean to sound harsh, but from our vantage point we can clearly see what needs to be accomplished and so many of you are stuck in your "why me" stories. "Why is this happening?" "Why them and not me?" Or, "Why is this happening to me and not to them?" Realize dear ones, that life is what you create it to be. If you do not realize this by now, then stop and re-read some of the previous Letters, particularly Letter 14. You will again see and hopefully come to realize with real-eyes that have a new perspective, that you are encountering these challenges for your own Soul's growth. Understand that it is not for the reason that God doesn't love you or that life is not in full support of what you are doing.

The relationship between yourself and Spirit is one in which openness and subtlety abound. Sometimes, but vary rarely, does Spirit make such a grand appearance that it would be considered a visual miracle witnessed by the multitudes. Moreover, Spirit works in the silence and is more personalized to subtlety work with the issues you are dealing with at the level in which you presently reside.

What must be said here is that Spirit cannot enter where it is not wanted and not believed in. If that is the case, it might be better to find another avenue to work out your difficulties. Spirit is here and will continue to be here should you decide to change your mind and open your heart.

For those of you that continue to read on, a open heart and mind are all that is required. Period. That is all. If you give us a chance, just the smallest opening in your heart, to show that Spirit is active and abundant in your life, we will. We might come to you in a song that answers a question that you have before you. We might come to you in a observation you just had that's different from the type of thoughts you had before. It might be the smallest change in perception about a topic or subject that grants itself expansion of perception - a perception you didn't hold until you opened your heart to us. It might come to you in a "hello" from a friendly stranger passing by. It might take its form in a field as the winds gently move upon the vegetation.

If you ask we will come. No, this is not The Field of Dreams movie but it is The Dream That is Your Life. We desire for you to dream. We desire, that you desire to dream. But dear ones, you must open your heart. You must set aside the stories that no longer serve you. Set aside the stories and the layers that are literally weighing you down. Cast them aside if only for a short time and give Spirit a chance to eventually show you what life is all about. We will make ourselves known to you. We will and do love you. Let us send our healing and loving energy. Let us wrap our light around you. Let us help. Give us a chance.

We ask that you Be Here Now. Be in this present moment and set aside what happened earlier today or yesterday or last month or last year. Pay no attention to what is supposed to happen later today or tomorrow or later this week or this month or year. To this present moment, those things are not important. Be fully present in this moment, open your heart and your mind. Take a deep breath and breathe slowly and calmly. Verbally invite Spirit, the Lord your God, the Creator of All of Life, however you know Him to be, into your life. Feel from your heart area, the energy of love being sent outward and feel the love being returned to you from the top of your head down through your entire body as though you are being bathed in a warm white light. Let that light envelope you and feel its safety and know its presence.

Say whatever you have to say to Spirit and watch your life develop a response. You will feel a resonance when the changes occur. You will resonate with something you read or something you hear or see and you will remember that Spirit has answered you. You will remember that there is no place in which Spirit is not. You will re-member. That is, you will have reactivated your membership with that part of you that is Divine and you will remember that you are one with all of life and with God.

This what we desire for you. For you to realize how great and special you are. We desire for you to see past your present situation and to look ahead at how wonderful and delicious your life is and can be. It is all here for you dear ones. It all begins with being open and willing. We are here waiting and we will continue to be here for you, for that is what love does.

We do love you so.

THE THIRTY SEVENTH LETTER

Who Am I?

You are Divinity.

You might not think of yourself as such, but it is true. You have left the realm of Spirit and have taken physical form in the realm of contrast. You are not your body, you are forever a spiritual being. You are an individualized aspect of The Source of All Things. The Source is Divine. Therefore, as an individualized aspect of Source, you are Divinity.

Does this clear up the matter? Does this answer all of your questions? No, it does not. In fact, we have just created new questions. In order for you to understand the vastness of who you are, a shift in perspective is necessary. You will have to change your thinking about yourself and you will have to let go of the judgements in which you have indicted yourself.

You see, in all of those moments in which you thought of yourself as less than you should be, in all of those times you thought you made a great mistake and those times you thought you were unworthy, were not as you supposed them to be. You see, your body was being used as a tool to gain wisdom through experience for the benefit of your Higher Self. Just as an artist would use a tool to sculpt and to create something to his liking, so has your Higher Self used your body and its experiences to do the same thing. You are a precious creation of art fashioned by your Higher Self. You, in your body, reading this Letter, are an aspect of your Higher Self or your Soul Self.

It is difficult to perceive this from your incarnate physical perspective. Especially if you are in the middle of a very difficult life experience. Believe us when we tell you that we understand. You must have the ability to rise outside of your current circumstance to be able to see your life from this vantage point. Meditation is a useful practice that will help you on your journey of self awareness and discovery.

What you are encountering right now is part of your Soul's plan to experience itself as it really is as it puts itself, through your body, in situations that it will benefit from. Take time for yourself in moments of quiet contemplation and meditation and you will soon discover a new way to view your current situation. You will come to see that you have a Higher Self. You will see that there is more to yourself than you previously understood. You will discover that you have uncharted depth. You will discover that you are a child of light - indeed you are from the light and eventually it is to the light to which you will return.

All of these bodily experiences are directed at moving you into the Higher Realms of existence. Each incarnation, each experience moves you closer to your Source and you take all of this experiential information and you once again, will create new experiences for yourself. You will create Higher experiences for yourself. You will create experiences in which you are able to love more, to forgive more, to give more and to be more. In order to experience all of this, it would not be possible unless you are able to experience the experiences you are undergoing and have undergone in this lifetime. Each experience builds on the next.

This is the life you have planned for yourself, dear one. Go forth and revel in the fact that you are Divine. Go forth with great joy and know that you are living your life with great purpose. Go with the knowledge that you are an individualized aspect of The Source of All Things. That you are an aspect of The Creator and as such were created in the image and likeness of The Creator. You are like what you came from. You are an Spiritual Eternal Creator Being having a physical existence at this point in time during your earth's history.

With this knowledge it is no doubt that you will create the world of your highest imaginings and we can't wait to watch you do it.

THE THIRTY EIGHTH LETTER

How Do I Find My Purpose?

At this time, we believe that your present system in which you manage your daily affairs might not be working well for you. Perhaps you can take a moment to examine how you spend your time. We would also like for you to determine whether you are happy when you engage in these activities. If you have answered "Yes," then we feel this portion is not relevant to you. We are then addressing those readers who believe that the time spent is not rewarding them with feelings of satisfaction and accomplishment. For those readers who are dissatisfied with their daily activities, we feel you have just begun to learn a new way to make yourselves be happier and lighter and more confident about yourselves. We can tell you that you are able to change your present state of activity-making and moving to a happier place than before you began reading this piece of literature.

So, we invite you to go to a place that is unfamiliar to you. We ask you to sit down now and consider creating more for yourself. How you will determine this is up to you. You will be able to chart a course that is new and vibrant so you can wake up in the morning and say, "I am ready to do this. I look forward to this new activity. I want to see myself doing that today. This is all I want for myself -- to be able to wake up and listen to my heart song tell me that my activities are rewarding and fun, and that I am making a difference for the world and all who occupy it."

We say to you that you can make a difference in the way you go into the world each day. You are a very special person and you contribute much in the way of offering your love and kindness and all you do that makes you unique to others. We see that you would love to shine more so we want you to know how to be able to do this here and now.

First, be as clear about who you are and what you wish to accomplish. Within reason, you can assume that the traits you possess are unique to others and what you can offer the world has the stamp of "This is Me and I'm The One in Charge of This Area of Life." It is this stamp that distinguishes you from others. Here is where the fun begins: You see yourself different in the ways that separate you from others. Now, go inside and ask yourself, "What makes me tick? How do I get motivated? What moves me to pieces? Why do I get so excited when I do certain things?" When you ask yourself these questions, you will come up with answers.

We know you will because you are getting to know yourself better and you are wanting to feel better. The answers that lie within you are many. You will probably have to write them down.

After you have written down your answers, the next step is a bit more involved. So, bear in mind that you are only beginning to see how great an impact you can make on the world and its inhabitants. Without this exercise that is a bit time consuming, you would not be able to come to these conclusions. Be kind to yourself, knowing that it is not so easy going from Point A to Point B in a flash. Sit back and let this process unfold. Okay?

So, here we are at the place where you have determined you have much to contribute, yet you are a bit unsure how to bring your gifts into the world for yourself each day. You might say to yourself, "Who cares what I do each day?" "Why am I to contribute to this world or to others, for that matter?" We say, "Because part of your job here is to provide us all, all over the world and beyond your grasp of what you see, with lovingkindness, acts of compassion, free will decisions regarding how you can improve situations so all involved can benefit, and so much more. Your job is to shine brightly on Humanity so that the inhabitants can feel that the world they live in is beautiful, peaceful, and worth living in." Do you see how important your job is?

We tell you this because we know that you are the maker of your own reality -- your daily reality, to be more specific. Each day that you live resembles a puzzle piece. When you put the puzzle pieces together, what will the puzzle picture look like? Will it be a perfect representation of your daily efforts that came together to make a smooth-finished photo, or will it look like a scrambled shot of someone who tried their best, but didn't put enough effort into the project? We believe that the picture you would wish to show others is the smooth one that shines your brightness -- your efforts of daily lovingkindness that were delivered each day to the world and the others around you.

From our perspective you are glimmering with hope -- hope for a better tomorrow. With this hope in your heart, you can come up with any project that suits you and that makes you feel that you can contribute to a great cause. You are worthy of a great many things, and supplying the world with your gifts is what makes you worthy of good things and all that comes with doing good for others. We know that you sit here and wonder what you can do. Each person can choose for them self what feels special and different about them, and then they can motivate themselves to, in turn, send out the energy, the work, and time commitment to share their gifts with others who share their lives.

We believe that this is a great undertaking. We believe that you have stumbled upon something here that is greater than you might know. We believe that there will be a day when you wake up each morning and feel that the reason you woke up was solely for the purpose of expanding beyond your present horizons -- to offer your gifts to the world and to others so that you all might feel that the world is truly a beautiful and wondrous place to reside. We believe that never more do you have to feel that what lies before you is despair and grief and suffering. All that is behind you now.

We know your hearts aches and we wish to soothe your wounds. We wish your hearts were fuller and that your grief was less. It is here we wish you our deepest and most heartfelt wishes of Peace and Love. For when you place our Peace and Love in the center of your heart, you will be able to manage more than before you did this. We understand the difficulties you experience. We know and we see what you have been holding inside yourselves. It is from our perspective that we believe you are able to move through your grief so you are able to consider making changes to your daily activities. We know this process will take a little time for you and we offer you our support here and now.

Know we are with you always. Our hearts beat as one at this moment in your Now. We see you and know you know we are here.

THE THIRTY NINTH LETTER

Does God Ever Say No?

Dear ones, In the most absolute terms God, the Source of All Things, is ever expansive. So the idea that God would say no to any request is not a possibility that can be entertained. But, for most of you at some time or another, you have had the experience of your heartfelt prayers go unanswered.

For many of you these were prayers of great desperation and we must tell you - we know. We know all of it. We could feel your heart break at times. We could feel your fear in a situation in which you thought there was no way out. And we have felt your emptiness during your losses.

What must be understood however is that there is a plan for your life. It was a plan made for you, by you for the expansion of your Soul and for the expansion of your Source. In all cases you encountered the exact circumstances that would lead you to great experiential learning that was necessary for your Soul's growth.

From your earthly perspective it feels as though your whole world was falling apart at times. Some of you have endured what seems like unending physical and emotional pain and abuse. Perhaps some of you are still going through some of these most difficult experiences. Your pleas for help have been heard and Angels have been sent to comfort you throughout your experience as many of you can attest.

What ultimately rings true however is the fact that the real you is not your body. Your body that is going through these difficult experiences is doing so for the benefit of the real you, your Higher Self or your Soul Self.

Your Soul seeks its completion in its experience and it draws from the experiences of itself in its human incarnation to give itself what it needs to expand. The expansion of the Soul is what the real you desires. And to do so, you enter into the realm of contrast and take human form, but it is not real. It's all made up and you place yourself into this theatrical play of sorts in which you are led through the experiences of your lifetime. When it is culminated in your last act, you can look back, sometimes even at the human level, and garner the rich diversity and grand lessons that you have learned. Many of these lessons could not have come about in any other way than the way they transpired, which was exactly the way you planned them to transpire prior to you entering into your physical existence.

You see, the Source Of All Things, has placed before each Soul the tools in which it needs to expand and to realize itself as its portion of Divinity. In this, God never says no, but gives full access to the universe in all its parts, so the Soul can reach its final destination with full reunification with God The Source. There it finds what it has yearned for and what it knew it always was, but had to experience itself as such.

You, dear ones are such a being. You are that portion of your Soul that is a portion of God. You are that portion of Divinity in Human form. It is with much love that you entered into this existence and that love continues throughout all of life's difficulties. It is even there when you think you can't feel it. It is always there as God is always there and neither will ever leave you for the love of God is always with you. To your precious Soul He never says no. He always says yes.

THE FORTIETH LETTER

How Can I Know That God Loves Me?

What you know now, you have always known. You just don't know that you know. Where you are from and where you are going, is one in the same. You will eventually end up home again. You will end up here where we are. It is where we are speaking from now. Watch us as we listen to you. You can do it. Close your eyes and let the vision unfold. Talk to us like you would talk to any other earthly friend. It's okay, really it is. Let your thoughts of today and tomorrow go. Let them fade away and ask your questions. Make your petitions and requests. Pour your heart out to us. It is okay. That is what we are here for, to listen, to feel, to guide and to assist. And assist you we will because that is what love does. Does it not?

When you were children you looked at a world full of glorious colors. You marveled at a world so wonderful at times it literally took your breath away. There were moments when you just couldn't take it and the joy within you welled up and then the tears came and they flowed freely because the emotion you felt was so tremendous. Many of you were grateful beyond compare. Many of you jumped for joy in these moments. We mean that you literally leaped in the air the charge of emotion was so great. And in these times, for most of you, you felt very taken care of. For most of you, you felt very watched over. And for most of you, you felt very loved. If one were to ask you within one of these heightened states if God loved you, there is no doubt that the answer would be a joyous YES, followed by a ear to ear grin.

But then, for many of you, the rains came and the seasons of your life changed. There were those times in most of your lives you would care to forget, but if you only could. These were the times when a grin on your face was the last thing on your mind. These were the times when you didn't want to go on. The pain was too great, the burden too much to carry and the scars that were too deep to ever heal. For some of you reading now, this is where you reside in the present moment. For some of you, you have moved past this and into a numbed state. Some of you have been so hurt, so bad, that you resigned yourself to the fact that this is really all there is, and by certain accounts, it doesn't appear that it's going to get better anytime soon.

We see you going through your anguished states and we again *feel* what you are going through. We can *feel* the anger, the hurt and frustration. We *feel* the bitterness and the hatred and yet we remain. We hear your cries, you pleas, your nasty comments and yet we remain. We remain through all of it, and by all accounts, we aren't leaving anytime soon.

Why? Why don't we just get up, turn our back and walk away (as if we have to walk)? We don't because, we love you. It was very easy for you to see God in the great moments of your life, but not so easy to see God within the pieces of your broken life while you try to navigate your way with only a broken heart to guide you. This is where life is dear ones. This is what life is. It is within the highest of highs and the lowest of lows. And yet we remain through all of it.

For some of you going through the low valleys of life right now, we would like you to see us in it with you. That's right, close your eyes, take a deep breath and exhale slowly. Visualize what you believe we look like on the other side. Think about God's face, if He had one, what would He look like? What would His Angels look like? What would His Guides and Messengers look like? Visualize all of us standing around you encompassing you in every direction. Visualize yourself standing there holding your problems in your hands and look at each one of us. Feel our love for you as you stare into our eyes. Feel our warmth and our gratitude for you and feel that there is our love for you without judgement and without measure.

We now ask you to consider that these same Angels and Guides have always been here. We ask you to realize that God has always been here, whether you feel Him or not. We have encompassed you from your first day here on earth, and by all accounts, we are not leaving anytime soon.

You see dear ones, we love you. We will never leave you. Why would we? How could we? You are one of us and we are you. We are of the same origin and to deny you would be to deny ourselves and we cannot do that. Our love for you is greater than you can comprehend right now. There are certain things within life on your planet that you have to see to believe. There are other things however, in which you have to *feel* your way through. We know that if you are truthful with yourself and you are able to set the problems of today aside for a moment, then you will be able to *feel* God's love for you and take away some of your anguish. His love is a Warm White Light that envelops you and you know that you are safe and and you know that you are loved.

You see dear ones, the inevitable has happened. There was always moments planned for you in which you realized the deep love that your Creator has for you. The deep love that we have for you. This love has always been surrounding you and it will always surround you, and by all accounts, we don't see that changing anytime soon.

From our heart to yours - because we share the same Spirit within our heart - We love you. God loves you. We ask you to *feel* our love now.

EPILOGUE

Congratulations.

What a glorious day. What a marvelous time to be alive. The universe is yours, enjoy it. Enjoy every moment in it, for all the moments strung together create your life as you know it. Enjoy each and every one. That is- bring that joy into you and make it a part of your being.

Throughout this series of Letters we have given you insights on how life works on your planet. We have given you insights into why your life is the way it is. We have given you directions to change your life, if your life isn't what you desire it to be. Can there yet be more to learn? Are there new opportunities waiting to be discovered? Of course there are. You can learn about densities and dimensions. You can learn about the subtleties of life and how powerful these subtleties are. You can engage even more in the expansiveness of the eternal Soul. There is always more to learn and experience.

For now, our purposes and intentions have been met. This series of Letters will serve humanity well for where it is presently in this time line. These Letters will serve Humanity in the form that is required. There is much work to do for Humanity to rise up and to reach its full potential, but you will do it. We know that if you place your intention on such acts of human grandeur, then you will achieve them. Never give up the hope that things can always get better. Never give up what you have learned here and the wisdom you have gained in reading our words.

We encourage you to read through this book several times and each time you will glean something new. Each exploration through this hall of knowledge will enlighten your physical self. The instruction may seem so very simple and it really is, but you would be surprised to know how many of the simple things you ignore. Life on your planet can be convoluted at times. The most important things for ones happiness have been substituted for that which does not serve you. This happens within a broad range of areas and subjects and we do not mean to suggest anything specific. But rather, we ask that you slow down and rest. We ask that the Human Race stop racing. We ask that you return to yourselves again. We ask that you ask questions, big questions, then help each other to find the answers. In doing so you will build yourself up. Better yet, you will build each other up.

Who will you be next? What new version of you will you create for yourself after you have considered what is written here? What you chose for you, we chose for you. If you chose your Highest potential, we would hope you chose that for others as well. Never forget that what you do for another you do for yourself. That is because you are all connected. You are all individual aspects of Divinity and Divinity runs through each and every one of you.

Never forget to love one another as we have loved you. We have reached out to you to lift you up. We have reached out to you to take you to a higher place. We have done this because we love you so. We have done this because - *this is what love does*. We ask that you do this for one another. Do this and together you will build a planet of never ending beauty and bounty. Do this and you will have created your Heaven on Earth. Indeed you are on your way.

As your fellow travelers, we wish you well.

We go now in peace.

This is so.

ABOUT THE AUTHOR

Brett L. Bowden is a metaphysician and spiritual channel for Divine wisdom. He works primarily through his guide Jaipur. He was contacted in 2007 by his Spirit Guides and given valuable information to pass onto the larger portion of Humanity. The information given pertain to a rebuilding of the planet through the rebuilding of the person.

If you have enjoyed Letters From Your Future, please take a moment and rate and review the book at one of the book selling websites or blogs. Your discussion of the book and its contents will ensure that others discover the treasures for Humanity within its pages.

For more from The Letters Project, please visit:
www.lettersfromyourfuture.com or
www.facebook.com/lettersfromyourfuture

Brett Bowden can be reached at
lettersfromyourfuture@gmail.com

Notes